W9-DFY-205

LOTUS® SMARTSUITE® MILLENNIUM EDITION FOR DUMMIES®

Quick Reference

by Joyce J. Nielsen

IDG BOOKS WORLDWIDE

IDG Books Worldwide, Inc.
An International Data Group Company

Foster City, CA ✦ Chicago, IL ✦ Indianapolis, IN ✦ New York, NY

Lotus® SmartSuite® Millennium Edition For Dummies® Quick Reference

Published by
IDG Books Worldwide, Inc.
An International Data Group Company
919 E. Hillsdale Blvd.
Suite 400
Foster City, CA 94404
www.idgbooks.com (IDG Books Worldwide Web site)
www.dummies.com (Dummies Press Web site)

Copyright © 1998 IDG Books Worldwide, Inc. All rights reserved. No part of this book, including interior design, cover design, and icons, may be reproduced or transmitted in any form, by any means (electronic, photocopying, recording, or otherwise) without the prior written permission of the publisher.

Library of Congress Catalog Card No.: 98-86182

ISBN: 0-7645-0405-3

Printed in the United States of America

10 9 8 7 6 5 4 3 2 1

1P/RU/QY/ZY/IN

Distributed in the United States by IDG Books Worldwide, Inc.

Distributed by Macmillan Canada for Canada; by Transworld Publishers Limited in the United Kingdom; by IDG Norge Books for Norway; by IDG Sweden Books for Sweden; by Woodslane Pty. Ltd. for Australia; by Woodslane (NZ) Ltd. for New Zealand; by Addison Wesley Longman Singapore Pte Ltd. for Singapore, Malaysia, Thailand, Indonesia and Korea; by Norma Comunicaciones S.A. for Colombia; by Intersoft for South Africa; by International Thomson Publishing for Germany, Austria and Switzerland; by Toppan Company Ltd. for Japan; by Distribuidora Cuspide for Argentina; by Livraria Cultura for Brazil; by Ediciencia S.A. for Ecuador; by Ediciones ZETA S.C.R. Ltda. for Peru; by WS Computer Publishing Corporation, Inc., for the Philippines; by Unalis Corporation for Taiwan; by Contemporanea de Ediciones for Venezuela; by Computer Book & Magazine Store for Puerto Rico; by Express Computer Distributors for the Caribbean and West Indies. Authorized Sales Agent: Anthony Rudkin Associates for the Middle East and North Africa.

For general information on IDG Books Worldwide's books in the U.S., please call our Consumer Customer Service department at 800-762-2974. For reseller information, including discounts and premium sales, please call our Reseller Customer Service department at 800-434-3422.

For information on where to purchase IDG Books Worldwide's books outside the U.S., please contact our International Sales department at 650-655-3200 or fax 650-655-3297.

For information on foreign language translations, please contact our Foreign & Subsidiary Rights department at 650-655-3021 or fax 650-655-3281.

For sales inquiries and special prices for bulk quantities, please contact our Sales department at 650-655-3200 or write to the address above.

For information on using IDG Books Worldwide's books in the classroom or for ordering examination copies, please contact our Educational Sales department at 800-434-2086 or fax 317-596-5499.

For press review copies, author interviews, or other publicity information, please contact our Public Relations department at 650-655-3000 or fax 650-655-3299.

For authorization to photocopy items for corporate, personal, or educational use, please contact Copyright Clearance Center, 222 Rosewood Drive, Danvers, MA 01923, or fax 978-750-4470.

LIMIT OF LIABILITY/DISCLAIMER OF WARRANTY: AUTHOR AND PUBLISHER HAVE USED THEIR BEST EFFORTS IN PREPARING THIS BOOK. IDG BOOKS WORLDWIDE, INC., AND AUTHOR MAKE NO REPRESENTATIONS OR WARRANTIES WITH RESPECT TO THE ACCURACY OR COMPLETENESS OF THE CONTENTS OF THIS BOOK AND SPECIFICALLY DISCLAIM ANY IMPLIED WARRANTIES OF MERCHANT-ABILITY OR FITNESS FOR A PARTICULAR PURPOSE. THERE ARE NO WARRANTIES WHICH EXTEND BEYOND THE DESCRIPTIONS CONTAINED IN THIS PARAGRAPH. NO WARRANTY MAY BE CREATED OR EXTENDED BY SALES REPRESENTATIVES OR WRITTEN SALES MATERIALS. THE ACCURACY AND COM-PLETENESS OF THE INFORMATION PROVIDED HEREIN AND THE OPINIONS STATED HEREIN ARE NOT GUARANTEED OR WARRANTED TO PRODUCE ANY PARTICULAR RESULTS, AND THE ADVICE AND STRAT-EGIES CONTAINED HEREIN MAY NOT BE SUITABLE FOR EVERY INDIVIDUAL. NEITHER IDG BOOKS WORLDWIDE, INC., NOR AUTHOR SHALL BE LIABLE FOR ANY LOSS OF PROFIT OR ANY OTHER COM-MERCIAL DAMAGES, INCLUDING BUT NOT LIMITED TO SPECIAL, INCIDENTAL, CONSEQUENTIAL, OR OTHER DAMAGES.

Trademarks: All brand names and product names used in this book are trade names, service marks, trademarks, or registered trademarks of their respective owners. IDG Books Worldwide is not associated with any product or vendor mentioned in this book.

 is a trademark under exclusive license to IDG Books Worldwide, Inc., from International Data Group, Inc.

About the Author

Joyce J. Nielsen is an author and consultant who writes and edits books, primarily based on Windows applications. She is the author or co-author of more than 25 computer books and has edited hundreds more. Prior to her work as a consultant, Joyce worked in product development for a computer book publisher. She also worked as a research analyst for a shopping mall developer, where she developed and documented computer applications used nationwide. She received a Bachelor of Science degree in Quantitative Business Analysis from Indiana University. Joyce recently relocated to sunny Tucson, Arizona to be closer to family and to escape the Indiana winters. (Unfortunately, she arrived in Arizona just in time for El Niño!) You can contact her via the Internet at joycen@azstarnet.com.

ABOUT IDG BOOKS WORLDWIDE

Welcome to the world of IDG Books Worldwide.

IDG Books Worldwide, Inc., is a subsidiary of International Data Group, the world's largest publisher of computer-related information and the leading global provider of information services on information technology. IDG was founded more than 25 years ago and now employs more than 8,500 people worldwide. IDG publishes more than 275 computer publications in over 75 countries (see listing below). More than 90 million people read one or more IDG publications each month.

Launched in 1990, IDG Books Worldwide is today the #1 publisher of best-selling computer books in the United States. We are proud to have received eight awards from the Computer Press Association in recognition of editorial excellence and three from *Computer Currents'* First Annual Readers' Choice Awards. Our best-selling *...For Dummies®* series has more than 50 million copies in print with translations in 38 languages. IDG Books Worldwide, through a joint venture with IDG's Hi-Tech Beijing, became the first U.S. publisher to publish a computer book in the People's Republic of China. In record time, IDG Books Worldwide has become the first choice for millions of readers around the world who want to learn how to better manage their businesses.

Our mission is simple: Every one of our books is designed to bring extra value and skill-building instructions to the reader. Our books are written by experts who understand and care about our readers. The knowledge base of our editorial staff comes from years of experience in publishing, education, and journalism — experience we use to produce books for the '90s. In short, we care about books, so we attract the best people. We devote special attention to details such as audience, interior design, use of icons, and illustrations. And because we use an efficient process of authoring, editing, and desktop publishing our books electronically, we can spend more time ensuring superior content and spend less time on the technicalities of making books.

You can count on our commitment to deliver high-quality books at competitive prices on topics you want to read about. At IDG Books Worldwide, we continue in the IDG tradition of delivering quality for more than 25 years. You'll find no better book on a subject than one from IDG Books Worldwide.

IDG BOOKS WORLDWIDE

John Kilcullen
CEO
IDG Books Worldwide, Inc.

Steven Berkowitz
President and Publisher
IDG Books Worldwide, Inc.

*Eighth Annual
Computer Press
Awards ≥1992*

*Ninth Annual
Computer Press
Awards ≥1993*

*Tenth Annual
Computer Press
Awards ≥1994*

*Eleventh Annual
Computer Press
Awards ≥1995*

IDG Books Worldwide, Inc., is a subsidiary of International Data Group, the world's largest publisher of computer-related information and the leading global provider of information services on information technology. International Data Group publishes over 275 computer publications in over 75 countries. More than 90 million people read one or more International Data Group publications each month. International Data Group's publications include: ARGENTINA: Buyer's Guide, Computerworld Argentina, PC World Argentina; AUSTRALIA: Australian Macworld, Australian PC World, Australian Reseller News, Computerworld, IT Casebook, Network World, Publish, Webmaster; AUSTRIA: Computerwelt Osterreich, Networks Austria, PC Tip Austria; BANGLADESH: PC World Bangladesh; BELARUS: PC World Belarus; BELGIUM: Data News; BRAZIL: Annuário de Informática, Computerworld, Connections, Macworld, PC Player, PC World, Publish, Reseller News, Supergamepower; BULGARIA: Computerworld Bulgaria, Network World Bulgaria, PC & MacWorld Bulgaria; CANADA: CIO Canada, Client/Server World, ComputerWorld Canada, InfoWorld Canada, NetworkWorld Canada, WebWorld; CHILE: Computerworld Chile, PC World Chile; COLOMBIA: Computerworld Colombia, PC World Colombia; COSTA RICA: PC World Centro America; THE CZECH AND SLOVAK REPUBLICS: Computerworld Czechoslovakia, Macworld Czech Republic, PC World Czechoslovakia; DENMARK: Communications World Danmark, Computerworld Danmark, Macworld Danmark, PC World Danmark, Techworld Denmark; DOMINICAN REPUBLIC: PC World Republica Dominicana; ECUADOR: PC World Ecuador; EGYPT: Computerworld Middle East, PC World Middle East; EL SALVADOR: PC World Centro America; FINLAND: MikroPC, Tietoverkko, Tietoviikko; FRANCE: Distributique, Hebdo, Info PC, Le Monde Informatique, Macworld, Reseaux & Telecoms, WebMaster France; GERMANY: Computer Partner, Computerwoche, Computerwoche Extra, Computerwoche FOCUS, Global Online, Macwelt, PC Welt; GREECE: Amiga Computing, GamePro Greece, Multimedia World; GUATEMALA: PC World Centro America; HONDURAS: PC World Centro America; HONG KONG: Computerworld Hong Kong, PC World Hong Kong, Publish in Asia; HUNGARY: ABCD CD-ROM, Computerworld Szamitastechnika, Internetto online Magazine, PC World Hungary, PC-X Magazin Hungary; ICELAND: Tolvuheimur PC World Island; INDIA: Information Communications World, Information Systems Computerworld, PC World India, Publish in Asia; INDONESIA: InfoKomputer PC World, Komputek Computerworld, Publish in Asia; IRELAND: Computerscope, PC Live!; ISRAEL: Macworld Israel, People & Computers/Computerworld; ITALY: Computerworld Italia, Macworld Italia, Networking Italia, PC World Italia; JAPAN: DTP World, Macworld Japan, Nikkei Personal Computing, OS/2 World Japan, SunWorld Japan, Windows NT World, Windows World Japan; KENYA: PC World East African; KOREA: Hi-Tech Information, Macworld Korea, PC World Korea; MACEDONIA: PC World Macedonia; MALAYSIA: Computerworld Malaysia, PC World Malaysia, Publish in Asia; MALTA: PC World Malta; MEXICO: Computerworld Mexico, PC World Mexico; MYANMAR: PC World Myanmar; NETHERLANDS: Computer! Totaal, LAN Internetworking Magazine, LAN World Buyers Guide, Macworld Netherlands, Net, WebWerld; NEW ZEALAND: Absolute Beginners Guide and Plain & Simple Series, Computer Buyer, Computer Industry Directory, Computerworld New Zealand, MTB, Network World, PC World New Zealand; NICARAGUA: PC World Centro America; NORWAY: Computerworld Norge, CW Rapport, Datamagasinet, Financial Rapport, Kursguide Norge, Macworld Norge, Multimediaworld Norge, PC World Ekspress Norge, PC World Nettverk, PC World Norge, PC World ProduktGuide Norge; PAKISTAN: Computerworld Pakistan; PANAMA: PC World Panama; PEOPLE'S REPUBLIC OF CHINA: China Computer Users, China Computerworld, China InfoWorld, China Telecom World Weekly, Computer & Communication, Electronic Design China, Electronics Today, Electronics Weekly, Game Software, PC World China, Popular Computer Week, Software Weekly, Software World, Telecom World; PERU: Computerworld Peru, PC World Profesional Peru, PC World SoHo Peru; PHILIPPINES: Click!, Computerworld Philippines, PC World Philippines, Publish in Asia; POLAND: Computerworld Poland, Computerworld Special Report Poland, Cyber, Macworld Poland, Networld Poland, PC World Komputer; PORTUGAL: Cerebro/PC World, Computerworld/Correio Informático, Dealer World Portugal, Mac*In/PC*In Portugal, Multimedia World; PUERTO RICO: PC World Puerto Rico; ROMANIA: Computerworld Romania, PC World Romania, Telecom Romania; RUSSIA: Computerworld Russia, Mir PK, Publish, Seti; SINGAPORE: Computerworld Singapore, PC World Singapore, Publish in Asia; SLOVENIA: Monitor; SOUTH AFRICA: Computing SA, Network World SA, Software World SA; SPAIN: Comunicaciones World España, Computerworld España, Dealer World España, Macworld España, PC World España; SRI LANKA: Infolink PC World; SWEDEN: CAP&Design, Computer Sweden, Corporate Computing Sweden, Internetworld Sweden, it.branschen, Macworld Sweden, MaxiData Sweden, MikroDatorn, Nätverk & Kommunikation, PC World Sweden, PCaktiv, Windows World Sweden; SWITZERLAND: Computerworld Schweiz, Macworld Schweiz, PCtip; TAIWAN: Computerworld Taiwan, Macworld Taiwan, NEW ViSiON/Publish, PC World Taiwan, Windows World Taiwan; THAILAND: Publish in Asia, Thai Computerworld; TURKEY: Computerworld Turkiye, Macworld Turkiye, Network World Turkiye, PC World Turkiye; UKRAINE: Computerworld Kiev, Multimedia World Ukraine, PC World Ukraine; UNITED KINGDOM: Acorn User UK, Amiga Action UK, Amiga Computing UK, Apple Talk UK, Computing, Macworld, Parents and Computers UK, PC Advisor, PC Home, PSX Pro, The WEB; UNITED STATES: Cadence, CIO Magazine, Computerworld, DOS World, Federal Computer Week, GamePro Magazine, InfoWorld, I-Way, Macworld, Network World, PC Games, PC World, Publish, Video Event, THE WEB Magazine, and WebMaster; online webzines: JavaWorld, NetscapeWorld, and SunWorld Online; URUGUAY: InfoWorld Uruguay; VENEZUELA: Computerworld Venezuela, PC World Venezuela; and VIETNAM: PC World Vietnam.   5/7/98

Author's Acknowledgments

Special thanks to Mary Bednarek and Mike Kelly for giving me the opportunity to write this book. Thanks also to my project editor, Ryan Rader, and to everyone behind the scenes at IDG Books Worldwide, Inc. for pulling everything together so smoothly!

Publisher's Acknowledgments

We're proud of this book; please register your comments through our IDG Books Worldwide Online Registration Form located at: http://my2cents.dummies.com.

Some of the people who helped bring this book to market include the following:

Acquisitions, Editorial, and Media Development

Project Editor: Ryan Rader

Acquisitions Manager: Michael Kelly

Copy Editors: Wendy Hatch, Tina Sims

Technical Editor: Steve Rindsberg

Editorial Manager: Elaine Brush

Editorial Assistant: Paul E. Kuzmic

Production

Project Coordinator: Karen York

Layout and Graphics: Lou Boudreau, Maridee V. Ennis, Angela F. Hunckler, Jane E. Martin, Brent Savage, Michael A. Sullivan

Proofreaders: Kelli Botta, Laura L. Bowman, Michelle Croninger, Rebecca Senninger, Janet M. Withers

Indexer: Sharon Duffy

Special Help: Linda S. Stark

General and Administrative

IDG Books Worldwide, Inc.: John Kilcullen, CEO; Steven Berkowitz, President and Publisher

IDG Books Technology Publishing: Brenda McLaughlin, Senior Vice President and Group Publisher

Dummies Technology Press and Dummies Editorial: Diane Graves Steele, Vice President and Associate Publisher; Mary Bednarek, Director of Acquisitions and Product Development; Kristin A. Cocks, Editorial Director

Dummies Trade Press: Kathleen A. Welton, Vice President and Publisher; Kevin Thornton, Acquisitions Manager

IDG Books Production for Dummies Press: Michael R. Britton, Vice President of Production and Creative Services; Beth Jenkins Roberts, Production Director; Cindy L. Phipps, Manager of Project Coordination, Production Proofreading, and Indexing; Kathie S. Schutte, Supervisor of Page Layout; Shelley Lea, Supervisor of Graphics and Design; Debbie J. Gates, Production Systems Specialist; Robert Springer, Supervisor of Proofreading; Debbie Stailey, Special Projects Coordinator; Tony Augsburger, Supervisor of Reprints and Bluelines

Dummies Packaging and Book Design: Robin Seaman, Creative Director; Jocelyn Kelaita, Product Packaging Coordinator; Kavish + Kavish, Cover Design

♦

The publisher would like to give special thanks to Patrick J. McGovern, without whom this book would not have been possible.

♦

Contents at a Glance

Table of Contents

How to Use This Book

Welcome to *Lotus SmartSuite Millennium Edition For Dummies Quick Reference*! If you're looking for a book that tells you just what you need to know — without extra fluff or technical stuff that you don't need — you've come to the right place. This book is for normal people who aren't concerned with all the intricacies of a software program and don't want to discover 12 different ways to do something. With this book, you can find the quickest, most efficient ways to accomplish tasks in Lotus SmartSuite Millennium Edition, and you may even make it home in time for dinner!

How This Book Is Organized

Because this *is* a quick reference, it obviously can't cover every feature in all the applications contained in SmartSuite. (That's actually not such a bad thing!) You will find that this book covers about 90 percent of the features that you'll ever use in SmartSuite Millennium Edition — unless you're a true guru, that is (in which case, you probably don't need to read this book).

This book skims through the most basic tasks fairly quickly. If you're new to computers or haven't used applications such as 1-2-3, Word Pro, or Freelance Graphics before, you may want to look for a book that describes many of the beginning tasks. If you need more details on how to get started with SmartSuite, pick up a copy of *Lotus SmartSuite Millennium Edition For Dummies,* by Michael Meadhra and Jan Weingarten (published by IDG Books Worldwide, Inc.).

Using this book as a reference

You probably won't be reading this book from cover to cover (unless you're a serious overachiever). *Lotus SmartSuite Millennium Edition For Dummies Quick Reference* is written as a reference that you can keep next to your computer, so that you can look up specific tasks and quickly figure out how to perform them. This book also serves as a refresher course for those who are experienced with SmartSuite Millennium Edition (or earlier versions of SmartSuite) but may have forgotten how to access a particular feature or task.

The tasks covered in each Part of this book are arranged alphabetically to allow you to easily locate the procedure you need. Of course, you can always turn to the Table of Contents and the Index to find specific information.

Looking at the Parts

Lotus SmartSuite Millennium Edition For Dummies Quick Reference is organized into nine different parts (without chapters).

Part I, "Getting to Know Lotus SmartSuite," provides a basic introduction to the components of SmartSuite Millennium Edition and lists some of the new features of this version.

Part II, "Common Tasks and Features," covers tasks that are common to all or most applications in SmartSuite Millennium Edition, such as opening files or getting help.

Parts III through VII are each devoted exclusively to a single application within SmartSuite — Lotus 1-2-3 (spreadsheet), Word

Pro (word processor), Freelance Graphics (presentations), Approach (database), and Organizer (personal information manager), respectively.

Part VIII, "Sharing Information among SmartSuite Applications," shows several ways that you can use the various SmartSuite applications together by sharing information between the programs.

In Part IX, "SmartSuite and the Web," you get to know the Web features — such as adding hyperlinks to SmartSuite documents and publishing data to the Web.

This book concludes with a Glossary of the most common terms that you're likely to encounter while using the SmartSuite applications. For more details on a specific term, look up the term in this book's Index.

Icon Alert!

As you flip through this book, funny-looking pictures, called *icons,* in the margins draw your attention to important information. The following icons are used in this book:

This icon draws attention to tidbits of information that may come in handy as you're performing a task.

Watch out! This icon warns you of things that can go wrong, such as data loss or unexpected events.

This icon indicates a quick alternative to accomplishing a task.

This icon highlights a feature or procedure that may not work as you would expect.

Other Helpful Features of This Book

In addition to the icons mentioned in the previous section, you also see pictures of *SmartIcons* in the margins of this book. SmartIcons are buttons that you click in various SmartSuite applications to perform common tasks quickly.

Many of the tasks in this book require that you use menu commands. These commands appear something like this:

Choose Edit⇨Copy.

This example indicates that you should open the Edit menu and then choose the Copy command. You can choose menu commands by using the keyboard or the mouse. The underlined characters indicate which letters in the command are keyboard hot keys (which are also used for dialog box options).

Keyboard shortcuts such as Ctrl+F2 are occasionally used in this book. This format indicates that you should press and hold down the first key (Ctrl, in this example) and then press the second key (F2, in this example).

Information that you need to type appears in **boldface** text. Names of check boxes, option buttons, and other options are spelled with the first letter of each word capitalized, even though those letters may not be capitalized on-screen. This convention changes the phrase "Check the Insert in a selected range only check box" into "Check the Insert In A Selected Range Only check box," which makes sentences filled with long option names easier to read.

Part 1

Getting to Know Lotus SmartSuite

Congratulations! If you're reading this book, you've already made a wise decision to use Lotus SmartSuite Millennium Edition to save time and increase your productivity. SmartSuite provides an integrated set of full-featured applications, all in one convenient package. You get a first-rate spreadsheet, word processor, database manager, presentation graphics program, and personal information manager, as well as a program for creating and maintaining Web sites and lots more. SmartSuite includes several powerful features that help you share information with others on a network or intranet or on the Internet. All of SmartSuite's applications and features work together seamlessly to help you simplify all your day-to-day computing tasks.

This part covers each of the major components in SmartSuite, as well as some slick new features that have been added to SmartSuite Millennium Edition.

In this part . . .

- ✔ Introducing the basics and the new features of the major SmartSuite applications
- ✔ Getting to know some other cool SmartSuite features

1-2-3

Lotus 1-2-3 is the spreadsheet component of SmartSuite Millennium Edition. Although you can use 1-2-3 for simple tasks such as performing basic math calculations or creating a budget, the real power of 1-2-3 lies in more complex analyses and lightning-fast data manipulation. You also can use 1-2-3 to create charts and geographical maps of your data, perform what-if analyses by saving and viewing different versions of your data in one file, create database tables, audit your worksheets, and publish 1-2-3 data to the Web.

The 1-2-3 worksheet consists of a large grid of columns and rows. The intersection of a column and row is called a *cell*. All your worksheet data — text, numbers, and formulas — is entered in worksheet cells. You can easily spruce up your worksheets to create a more professional appearance (and impress your boss!) by formatting the data. For example, you can change fonts and number formats, add borders or styles, apply different colors to text or cell backgrounds, and use attributes such as bold, italics, and underlining. Many common tasks in 1-2-3 can be performed quickly by clicking a SmartIcon (those buttons with pretty pictures near the top of the screen) or a button on the status bar (at the bottom of the screen).

The Millennium Edition of 1-2-3 includes some exciting new features:

✦ New Internet features that let you bring Web site data into 1-2-3 and refresh the linked data as needed, open and save HTML files, and create hyperlinks in your worksheets that link to objects in the same file, to objects in a different file, or to a location on the Internet.

✦ SmartLabels that automatically enter formulas or functions in your worksheets for you.

✦ New Help features, including Ask the Expert, which enables you to type your question and quickly find a solution, and the Microsoft Excel Menu Finder, which makes switching from Excel to 1-2-3 easy for you.

Check out Part III of this book for coverage of common 1-2-3 tasks.

Sheet tab

SmartIcons

Navigator┐ ┌Function selector   New sheet button

Edit line Title bar│   Menu bar   Tab scrollers┐

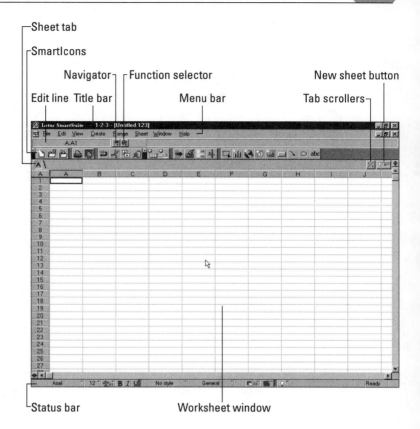

Status bar   Worksheet window

Word Pro

The word processing application in Lotus SmartSuite is called Word Pro. You can use Word Pro to create both business and personal documents such as letters, mailing labels, envelopes, newsletters, reports, brochures, and so on. Creating a Word Pro document is as simple as typing text in the document window. You can then use Word Pro to edit and format the text, check spelling and grammar, and change the page layout. You also can incorporate tables, drawings, charts, and graphics (such as clip art) in your Word Pro documents.

For lengthier documents, you can use Word Pro to add headers and footers, indexes, tables of contents, and footnotes. You also can track document revisions, compare documents, view documents using outline levels, and create numbered and bulleted lists. The SmartIcons and the buttons on the status bar enable you to perform common tasks quickly.

SmartIcons

Insertion point Title bar   Menu bar

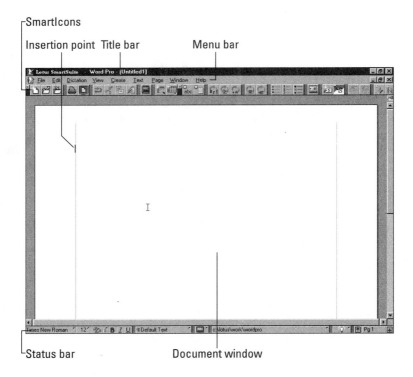

Status bar   Document window

New Word Pro features available in SmartSuite Millennium Edition include:

◆ IBM ViaVoice technology, voice-recognition software that you can use to dictate text into your Word Pro documents. You also can use ViaVoice to convert typed text into speech and to navigate menus without using the keyboard or the mouse.

◆ The Export Assistant, which quickly converts your Word Pro documents to HTML format for use on the Web.

◆ New Help features such as Ask the Expert, which enables you to type your question and quickly find a solution, and menu finders, which ease the transition from another word processor (Word, WordPerfect, or Ami Pro) to Word Pro.

You can find more information on Word Pro in Part IV of this book.

Freelance Graphics

Freelance Graphics is the presentation graphics application in SmartSuite. With Freelance Graphics, you can create dazzling presentations with minimum time and effort. The program includes dozens of SmartMaster templates, which include an array of pre-formatted pages created by graphic designers. You also can use content SmartMasters, which contain actual text that you can use as a starting point for creating business plans, project proposals, a corporate overview, and so on. If necessary, you also can start with a blank presentation and customize it to your own needs.

Although Freelance Graphics presentations are typically used for computer screen shows, you also can create overhead transparencies and printed pages. In addition, you can output to 35mm slides or transmit your presentation via the Internet. Freelance Graphics also enables you to add sound effects and transitions to your presentations.

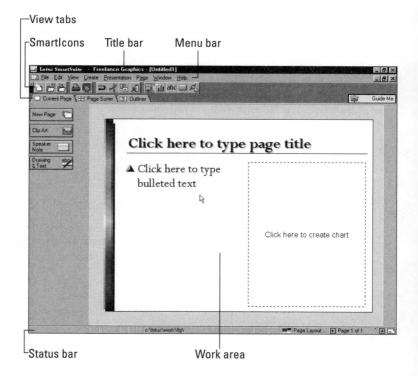

The Millennium Edition of Freelance Graphics includes these new features:

- ✦ New Internet features that enable you to convert presentation graphics to GIF or JPEG formats.

✦ The Convert to Web Pages Assistant, which converts your presentations to Web pages and optimizes them for fast downloading.

✦ The new Save and Go feature that compresses and saves your Freelance Graphics presentation (along with the Mobile Screen Show Player) to a floppy disk so that you can take it with you on the road.

Refer to Part V of this book for more information on Freelance Graphics.

Approach

Approach is the full-fledged database application in SmartSuite. With Approach, you can manage and organize a large quantity of related data, making it easier to find the information you need — when you need it. An Approach database can be as simple as a catalog of your favorite music CDs or as complex as an integrated accounting system created by a database administrator or programmer! Of course, most of us aren't programmers, so this book covers the basics you need to set up your Approach database, organize your data, and produce automated reports.

You don't always need to create a database from scratch. Approach includes several *SmartMasters,* which are ready-to-use database applications designed for both business and personal use. You can use these SmartMasters as they are or customize them to fit your own needs.

New Approach features in SmartSuite Millennium Edition include:

✦ New Internet features that let you save Approach data in jDoc format, which provides high-quality output to the Web.

✦ Compliance with IBM's Year 2000 standards, which ensures that Approach consistently interprets two-digit date entries for the 20th and 21st centuries.

✦ Enhanced SQL support that enables you to access and analyze SQL data more quickly than in previous versions of Approach.

Part VI of this book covers common tasks that you can perform by using Approach.

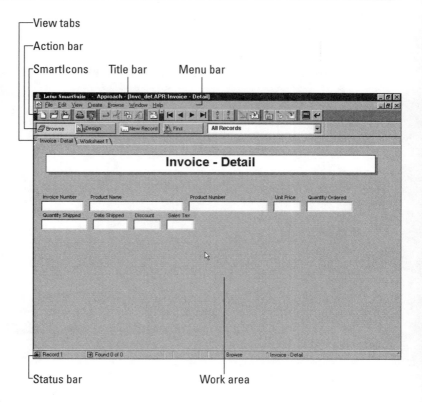

View tabs

Action bar

SmartIcons   Title bar   Menu bar

Status bar   Work area

Organizer

Lotus Organizer is a personal information manager (or *PIM,* in computerese). As the name implies, you can use this application to organize your appointments and activities, track and make phone calls, maintain an address list, keep notes, and plan future events. The work area in Lotus Organizer resembles a notebook with tabs for each section of the program: Calendar, To Do, Address, Calls, Planner, Notepad, and Anniversary. Just click the tab you want, and Organizer flips to that section. You can use the Toolbox or SmartIcons for one-click access to the most common Organizer commands and functions.

Today's date

Toolbox   Title bar   Menu bar   SmartIcons

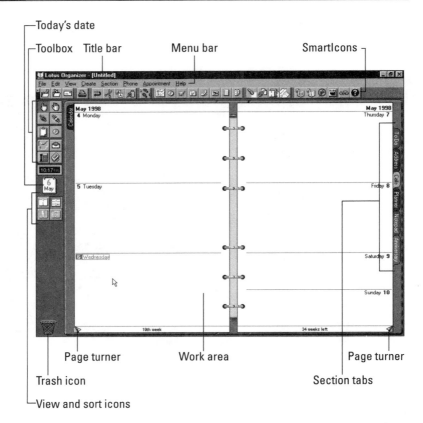

Page turner   Work area   Page turner

Trash icon   Section tabs

View and sort icons

New Organizer features in SmartSuite Millennium Edition include:

♦ New SmartIcons that provide direct connections to the OAG (Official Airline Guide) Travel Information System on the Web and to other Web pages that provide maps, directions, and online addresses.

♦ EasyClip, a tool that lets you copy information from another program or location (such as an e-mail message) directly into Organizer.

♦ Corex CardScan, which you can use to scan business cards into your address records in Organizer.

See Part VII of this book for more details on using Organizer.

Other SmartSuite Features

In addition to the five core applications, Lotus SmartSuite is jam-packed with other features to make you more productive than you ever thought possible. SmartSuite has so many features, in fact, that listing all of them in a book this size would be impossible. Here are some of the coolest SmartSuite features that you may want to investigate:

✦ **Lotus SmartCenter:** SmartCenter is the button bar that appears at the top of your screen. This feature gives you quick access to SmartSuite applications and files, Internet Web sites, Help information, a calendar and address book, reference information, and productivity tools. Each of the buttons on SmartCenter is called a *drawer*. You click a button to open a drawer and access folders and icons; then you click the button again to close the drawer. You can find out more about SmartCenter in Part II of this book.

✦ **Lotus FastSite:** FastSite is a new feature in SmartSuite Millennium Edition. FastSite enables you to convert your existing SmartSuite documents to Web pages, preview the Web pages, and then post the pages to a Web server. You can accomplish all of this without learning or using HTML! FastSite includes several professional-looking SmartMaster documents so that you don't need to spend hours of your time formatting your pages to make them look just right. Part IX of this book covers the details of using FastSite.

✦ **Lotus ScreenCam:** Because ScreenCam is a highly specialized feature used mostly for training purposes, this book doesn't cover all the details of using it. But ScreenCam is such a neat feature that it deserves a mention (so you'll at least know that it's there!). You can use Lotus ScreenCam to capture "movies" of your computer screen. If you're a computer trainer, for example, you can create a movie that records your on-screen movements and your voice, to be played back later. To open this application, choose Start⇨Programs⇨Lotus SmartSuite⇨Lotus ScreenCam.

Part II

Common Tasks and Features

One advantage of using Windows applications — particularly "suite" programs that work together, such as Lotus SmartSuite — is that several procedures and features are common across all or most applications. This standardization makes it easier for you to transfer your knowledge of the basic skills or features in one application to another program. This part covers common tasks in Windows applications (such as opening and saving files), as well as features found in multiple applications within SmartSuite.

In this part...

✔ **Opening, closing, saving, and deleting files**

✔ **Starting and closing programs**

✔ **Completing tasks**

✔ **Using common SmartSuite features**

✔ **Getting help**

Alternative Ways to Execute Commands

In Lotus SmartSuite, you can choose from several different ways to perform the same tasks. Some commands can be executed in five different ways:

✦ By using an InfoBox (which is a form of dialog box, discussed later in this section)

✦ By using a keyboard shortcut

✦ By using a command menu

✦ By clicking a SmartIcon

✦ By clicking a button on the status bar

For example, you can use all five of these different methods to apply boldface to selected text in Word Pro. However, not every command can be performed using each of these techniques — most commands can be carried out by using just a couple of the methods described above. Of course, you don't need to know every possible way to select a command in SmartSuite. You may prefer using the mouse to choose commands; or, if your hands are already on the keyboard, you may save time by using keyboard shortcuts.

Many commands in SmartSuite applications display dialog boxes prompting you for more information, but some commands (such as clicking the Bold button on the status bar) are carried out immediately in the file. Any menu command that leads to a dialog box is followed by an ellipsis (...) in the drop-down or shortcut (right-click) menus.

InfoBoxes

The InfoBox provides a fast way to change the properties of an object in the current file. An InfoBox includes multiple tabs, with related options on each tab, similar to some dialog boxes. Unlike a dialog box, however, you can keep the InfoBox open as you work. The changes you make by using the InfoBox are reflected immediately in the selected object.

You can use the InfoBox to change properties of the entire file (such as a document or worksheet), or a specific part of a file (such as a text selection, a range of cells, or a chart). The drop-down list at the top of an InfoBox allows you to specify which properties you want to change; the options that you see listed in this drop-down list vary depending on what's currently selected in the file. To get help on an option in the InfoBox, click the question

mark button (next to the Close button) in the InfoBox. A Help
window appears, displaying information on that particular tab of
the InfoBox. When you're finished using an InfoBox, click the Close
button (the X) in the upper right corner of the InfoBox.

The following figure shows the Font, Attribute, and Color tab of
the Range Properties InfoBox in 1-2-3.

Press Alt+Enter to quickly display an InfoBox. You can double-click
the title bar of the InfoBox to reduce its size, so that only the title
bar and tabs are visible. Click one of the InfoBox tabs to display
the entire InfoBox again and access the options on that tab. To
move an InfoBox, drag its title bar to another area of the screen.

Keyboard shortcuts

Some of the more common commands used in the SmartSuite
applications include *keyboard shortcuts*, also called shortcut keys.
For example, you can press Ctrl+S to save the current file (instead
of choosing the File⇨Save command), or Ctrl+F2 to check the
spelling in the current file. Many of the keyboard shortcuts are
listed in the drop-down menus, next to their corresponding
commands. For a complete listing of keyboard shortcuts that work
in a SmartSuite application, switch to that application and search
for "keyboard shortcuts" in the Help system. You can print the
Help listing for future reference.

Menu commands and shortcut menus

Nearly all commands in the SmartSuite applications are accessible
via the main menu, which appears just below the application's title
bar. To access a menu command, follow these steps:

1. Click one of the main menu options (such as File) and then
   click the command that you want from the drop-down menu.

2. Choose a subsequent menu item or specify your setting in a
   dialog box that may appear. (If the command in the drop-
   down menu is followed by an ellipsis, a dialog box appears
   when you select that command, enabling you to specify all the
   settings for that command. A command that's followed by a

right-pointing triangle leads to another level of menu commands. All other commands are carried out immediately when you click them.)

3. To leave a menu, press Escape one or more times, as necessary.

One of the main menu options may change in a SmartSuite application, depending on what you do. If you select a drawing in 1-2-3, for example, the Range main menu option is temporarily replaced with the Drawing main menu option. When you select a cell or range in the worksheet, the Range main menu option returns.

As with most other Windows applications, you also can use shortcut menus in SmartSuite. If you right-click an object, cell, or selection, a shortcut menu pops up. This shortcut menu lists commands that are useful for the current selection. Because of this, choosing menu commands from shortcut menus is often faster than searching for the command you want from the main menu in an application.

The following figure shows the shortcut menu that appears when you right-click a table in Freelance Graphics. Notice that the options listed in this menu relate to actions you perform on tables.

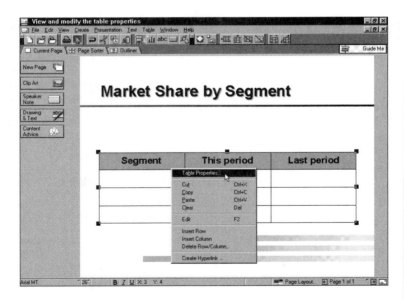

SmartIcon bar

Some of the most common commands that you use in a SmartSuite application (such as opening and printing files) can be performed by clicking one of the *SmartIcons* — the pictures that appear in a bar just below the main menu. Point to a SmartIcon to see a balloon containing a brief description of its function. You can display additional SmartIcon bars or change the SmartIcons that appear on existing bars. Pictures of SmartIcons appear in this book's margins to help you decide which SmartIcon to use for a particular procedure.

See also "SmartIcons," later in this part.

Status bar

The *status bar,* which appears at the bottom of the screen, includes buttons that provide quick access to formatting commands or other information relevant to the application. The buttons on the 1-2-3 and Word Pro status bars both relate primarily to formatting options (such as fonts, colors, styles, and attributes, including bold, italics, and underline). In Approach and Freelance Graphics, the status bars are quite different and feature buttons that are useful for those particular applications. Lotus Organizer doesn't include a status bar.

To use the status bar options, select the text (or cells) that you want to apply the format to (if applicable). Then click the button you want. If a pop-up menu or palette appears, select the desired option.

Closing a File

If you're finished working with a file but you want to keep the program open, you can close the file to remove it from the screen and get it out of your way. Closing a file doesn't permanently delete the file from disk — it just removes the file from memory. If you've made changes since you last saved the file, the program asks you whether you want to save the file before closing it. When you exit a program, you don't need to close individual files first — the files are automatically closed for you.

Use one of the following methods to close a file:

✦ Choose File➪Close.

✦ Click the Close button (the X) at the far right end of the menu bar. (If the document window isn't maximized, click the Close button in the upper-right corner of that window to close the file.)

Be careful when you click a Close button! The Close button at the right end of the menu bar exits the individual file, but the Close button at the right end of the title bar exits the program.

See also "Closing a Program," later in this part.

Closing a Program

When you're done using a SmartSuite program, you can close the application to free the memory that it uses. Use any one of the following methods to shut down the application:

✦ Choose File⇨Exit.

✦ Click the Close button (the X) at the far right end of the program's title bar.

✦ Press Alt+F4.

If you've modified any open files since you last saved them, a dialog box asks whether you want to save your changes. Click Yes to save the changes, Cancel to return to the file without exiting the program, or No to close the program without saving your recent changes.

You should *never* exit a SmartSuite program (or any other program, for that matter) by shutting off your computer. This can cause major problems such as data loss! Always exit all of your open applications and then shut down Windows before you turn off your computer.

Deleting a File

You can delete an entire SmartSuite file if you no longer need the file. The program always prompts you for confirmation before deleting the file from disk. You can't delete a file that's currently open — you must first close the file. Follow these steps to delete a file from within a SmartSuite application:

1. If the file you want to delete is open, close the file; then choose File⇨Open to display the Open dialog box.

2. In the list box of the Open dialog box, click the name of the file that you want to delete. If you don't see the file listed, select the drive and folder containing the file from the Look In drop-down list; then click the file name in the list box.

3. Press the Delete key on your keyboard.

4. Click Yes to delete the file and send it to the Recycle Bin, or No to cancel the delete operation.

Remember that if you delete a file by accident, you can recover it from the Recycle Bin in Windows. To do so, double-click the Recycle Bin icon on your desktop. In the Recycle Bin window, click the name of the file that you want to recover and then choose File⇨Restore.

Help Information

SmartSuite provides lots of different ways for you to get help in an application. The Millennium Edition of SmartSuite now includes an "Ask the Expert" feature that enables you to type specific questions and find the help you need in 1-2-3 and Word Pro. In addition, you can find help via the Help Topics dialog box, online application manuals, QuickDemos, menu finders, and the Internet.

Accessing the application manuals

If you purchased the CD-ROM version of SmartSuite, you can access detailed manuals about the SmartSuite applications. These manuals can be viewed and printed by using Adobe Acrobat Reader 3.0, which is included with SmartSuite Millennium Edition. If you used a typical (default) installation, the manuals are located on your hard disk. If you used a custom install and chose not to install the manuals, you can access them directly from the CD-ROM.

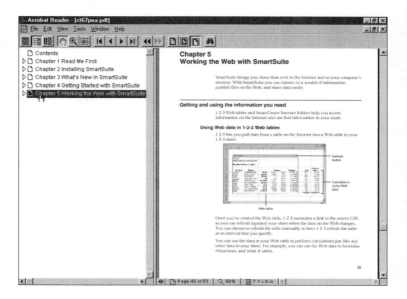

Follow these steps to display a manual about one of the SmartSuite applications:

1. Choose Start⇨Programs⇨Lotus SmartSuite⇨Lotus DocOnline.

2. Select the option corresponding to the manual that you want to view. Lotus uses Adobe Acrobat Reader 3.0 to display the file.

3. Read the information and then click the Close button in the Acrobat Reader window when you're done.

You can print information that appears in an application manual. From Adobe Acrobat Reader, choose File⇨Print. In the Print Range area of the Print dialog box that appears, specify the range of pages that you want to print and then click OK to begin printing.

If you used a custom installation and chose not to install these manuals to your hard disk, you can access them directly from the CD-ROM whenever you want to refer to them. (You may prefer this method if your hard disk space is limited.) Follow these steps:

1. Insert the SmartSuite CD in your CD-ROM drive.

2. In Lotus SmartCenter, open the Suite Help drawer; then click the DocOnline folder.

3. Double-click the icon representing that manual you want to open. Lotus uses Adobe Acrobat Reader 3.0 to display the file.

4. Read the information and then click the Close button in the Acrobat Reader window when you're done.

If you're not familiar with how to use Adobe Acrobat Reader, choose Help⇨Reader Online Guide (while you're in that application) to view extensive Help information on the program.

Accessing the product update information

Lotus provides product update information with your software that's more recent than what appears in your online Help Topics dialog box and the application manuals. To view the product updates, follow these steps:

1. Choose Start⇨Programs⇨Lotus SmartSuite⇨Lotus User Assistance.

2. Select the option corresponding to the update information you want to view (such as Freelance Product Updates). Lotus displays the appropriate README file in a WordPad window.

3. Read the information and then click the Close button in the WordPad window when you're done.

To print the product update information, display the file in WordPad (as explained in the preceding steps). Then choose File⇨Print, specify the print options, and click OK.

Ask the Expert feature

The Ask the Expert feature is available in 1-2-3 and Word Pro. The Expert enables you to type your question in your own wording to find topics relating to your question. You can access this feature quickly from the status bar. Follow these steps in 1-2-3 or Word Pro:

1. Click the Expert button (the light bulb) in the status bar. (You also can choose Help⇨Ask the Expert.) The Expert pop-up window appears, with a list of tasks displayed.

2. If the list doesn't display the task that you want, type your question in the list box and then click the Ask button.

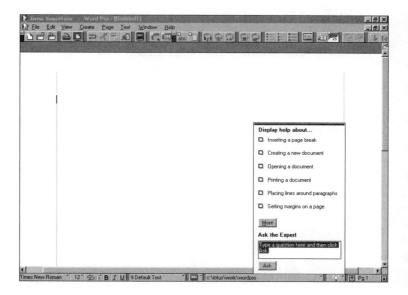

3. A list of tasks relating to your question appears in the Expert pop-up window. You can click the More button to see additional tasks, if applicable. Click the topic that you want, and the appropriate Help window appears.

4. When you're finished with the Help window, click the Close button.

Help Topics dialog box

Help Topics is the familiar dialog box that you've probably used in previous versions of SmartSuite or in other Windows applications. To display this dialog box, choose Help⇨Help Topics. (If a message dialog box appears, click the Help Topics button to display the Help Topics dialog box.) The Help Topics dialog box displays three tabs, as shown in the following figure. Click one of the tabs to find the Help information you need. To print a Help topic, click the Print button near the top of the Help window.

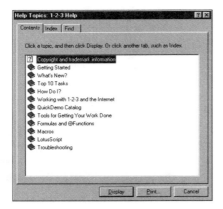

The Help Topics tabs serve the following purposes:

✦ **Contents:** Use this tab to browse through a short list of Help topics. Double-click a book icon to expand the topic and see more specific Help topics.

✦ **Index:** In the text box of the Index tab, type the name of the feature for which you want help. When you see the topic that you want in the list box, click the topic and then click the Display button.

✦ **Find:** If you don't know the name of a feature or task, use this tab to search for specific words or phrases in the Help system. If you haven't used this tab before, you need to follow the steps in the Find Setup Wizard to allow Find to create a list of words from the Help files. This process may take several minutes. When the Find tab appears, follow the step-by-step instructions on the tab to locate the topic that you want.

For more comprehensive help on general SmartSuite tasks and procedures that involve multiple applications (such as copying 1-2-3 data to a Word Pro document), access the Help Topics feature from SmartCenter. Click the Lotus button at the left end of the SmartCenter bar and choose Help Topics. The Help Topics dialog box appears.

Internet support

If you have access to the Internet from your computer, you can obtain Help information directly from the Lotus Customer Support site on the Web. Here, you may be able to find more current information on the product for which you have a question. Follow these steps to access Lotus Customer Support on the Web:

1. From within a SmartSuite application, choose Help⇨Lotus Internet Support⇨Lotus Customer Support. Your browser opens and displays the Lotus Customer Support home page.

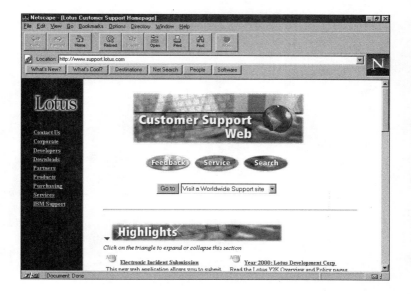

2. Follow the links on the Web page to find the information that you need. Then, if desired, exit your browser and disconnect from the Internet when you're done.

See also Part IX, "SmartSuite and the Web," for more information on Web topics.

QuickDemos

QuickDemos provide animated help for common procedures within SmartSuite applications. To start a QuickDemo, click the QuickDemo icon that appears in a Help window.

You can use QuickDemos in 1-2-3 and Word Pro as follows:

✦ To see a list of the QuickDemos that are available in 1-2-3, choose Help⇨QuickDemos. In the Help window that appears, choose the QuickDemo you want to view.

✦ To find the QuickDemos in Word Pro and Approach, search for "QuickDemos" in the Help Topics dialog box. ***See also*** "Help Topics dialog box," earlier in this section.

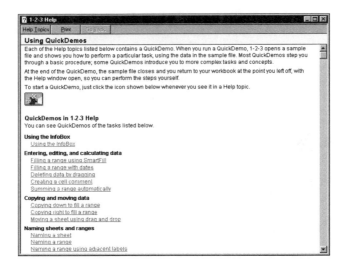

When you run a QuickDemo, a sample file opens, and QuickDemo performs the steps that appear in the Help window. The sample file closes at the end of the QuickDemo, and you're returned to your file. The Help window remains open so that you can then perform the steps yourself.

To view demos in Freelance Graphics, you use a slightly different procedure for a feature called Guide Me. Follow these steps:

1. Click the Guide Me button near the upper-right corner of the window (or choose Help⇨Guide Me).

2. From the resulting list, select the task for which you need help. A Help window appears with instructions on performing the task. If animated help is available, you see an icon labeled "Show me a demo."

3. When you're finished, click the Close button in the Help window.

Using the menu finders

Both 1-2-3 and Word Pro provide help for users who are making the transition from another spreadsheet or word processor. 1-2-3 provides help for Excel users, and Word Pro includes help for Word, WordPerfect, and Ami Pro users. This feature enables you to find out which menu commands to use in 1-2-3 and Word Pro to carry out tasks that you performed in the other spreadsheet or word processor.

Follow these steps to use the Excel menu finder in 1-2-3:

1. Choose Help⇨Microsoft Excel Menu Finder. The Excel Menu Finder window appears.

2. Choose an Excel command from the menu at the top of the window. The comparable 1-2-3 command appears inside the yellow box.

3. Click the Close button to close the menu finder.

The menu finders in Word Pro work a bit differently. In Word Pro, use these steps to access the menu finders:

1. Choose Help from the main menu and then select one of the following:

- Ami Pro Menu Help

- Microsoft Word Menu Help

- For WordPerfect Users⇨WordPerfect Win Menu Help

2. A menu (from the word processor that you chose in Step 1) appears under the Select a Menu Item title bar. From this menu, choose the command from Ami Pro, Word, or WordPerfect that you want to look up.

3. Word Pro lists one or more possible command equivalents in the list box. Double-click the item in the list box that most closely matches what you're looking for. A Word Pro Help window appears with steps on how to perform the task.

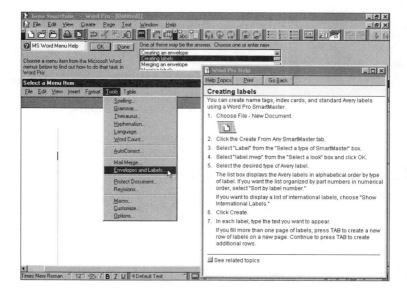

4. When you're finished with the menu finder, click the Done button. You can keep the Help window open as you complete the steps in Word Pro. Then click the Close button to close the Help window.

When all else fails . . . (Lotus Customer Support)

Have you searched through all the on-screen and online Help information and still can't find what you're looking for? You can get the help you need by contacting a real, *live* person at Lotus Customer Support. There are lots of different numbers you can call, depending on your situation and where you live. You find the Lotus Customer Support numbers that you need in SmartSuite's Help system.

From any of the SmartSuite applications, select Help⇨Help Topics and click the Contents tab. Double-click the Troubleshooting option and then double-click Lotus Customer Support. Continue double-clicking the appropriate categories until you find the information and phone number that you need.

If you have access to the Internet from your computer, you also can connect to Lotus Customer Support on the Web. From a SmartSuite application, choose Help⇨Lotus Internet Support⇨ Lotus Customer Support.

Opening a File

After you save a file to disk, you'll most likely want to open the file again later to make changes to the file or print the data. Opening a file loads the file into memory; any changes you make to the file should be saved if you want to keep those changes. *See* **also** "Saving a File," later in this part.

In most cases, you use the Open dialog box to open an existing file. If you've used the file recently, you may be able to select the file name directly from the bottom of the application's File menu.

Display the Open dialog box by using one of the following methods:

♦ Click the Open an Existing File SmartIcon.

♦ Choose File➪Open.

♦ Press Ctrl+O.

Follow these steps when you see the Open dialog box:

1. In the Look In drop-down list, select the drive and folder containing the file that you want to open.

2. Click the file name in the list box and then click Open to open the file.

To open multiple files at the same time in 1-2-3 or Word Pro (without re-opening the Open dialog box for each file), follow these steps:

1. In the Open dialog box, click the first file that you want to open.

2. Hold down the Ctrl key and click each additional file that you want to open.

3. Click the Open button to open all the selected files.

When you start a SmartSuite application, you may see a Welcome dialog box. From this dialog box, you can open files that you've recently used. Click the Open an Existing Document (or Workbook or Presentation) tab, select the file in the list box, and click OK.

To open a new file in a SmartSuite application (instead of using an existing file), click the Create a New File SmartIcon. If you start a SmartSuite application and the Welcome dialog box appears, you also can click the Create button at the bottom of the dialog box to immediately open a blank document.

Saving a File

When you create a new file or modify an existing file, the changes that you make aren't permanent until you save the file. What happens if you shut down your applications before saving your files? You lose all the work that you did since the last time you saved the file (*if* you saved it at all!).

Be sure to save your work frequently to avoid accidental data loss. You never know when you might experience a power outage, or when your computer might lock up. (The latter actually happened to me as I was writing this section! Luckily, I had recently saved my work, so I didn't lose much data.)

Use any one of the following methods to save the current file to disk:

♦ Click the Save the Current File SmartIcon.

♦ Choose File⇨Save.

♦ Press Ctrl+S.

If you save a file that has previously been saved, the file in memory automatically replaces the file with the same name on disk.

If the file hasn't been saved yet, the program displays the Save As dialog box and prompts you to enter a file name. You also see this dialog box if you choose File⇨Save As to save an existing file with a new file name.

Follow these steps to save by using the Save As dialog box:

1. In the Save In drop-down list, select the drive and folder where you want to save the file.

2. Type a name for the file in the File Name text box. (If you want to rename an existing file, type a new file name here.)

3. Click the Save button.

To save your file in a different file format, use the Save As Type drop-down list in the Save As dialog box. You may choose to do this, for example, if you need to exchange files with coworkers who use an earlier version of the program.

You may lose some formatting or other file information if you save to an older file format. If this occurs, the SmartSuite application displays a dialog box to warn you of the possible loss. This normally happens if you use features or commands in an application that aren't available in the older version of that application. When you save a file to an older file format, be sure to change the file name so that you can always revert to your original file.

See also " Publishing SmartSuite Data to the Web" in Part IX.

SmartCenter

You can think of SmartCenter as the control center of Lotus SmartSuite. SmartCenter is the button bar at the top of your screen. (If you don't see SmartCenter on your screen, choose Start⇨Programs⇨Lotus SmartSuite⇨Lotus SmartCenter.) From SmartCenter, you can access all the SmartCenter applications, specific files that you've worked on, Internet sites, and Help information. In addition, SmartCenter provides quick access to a calendar, address book, reminders, reference information, and business productivity tools.

Opening SmartCenter drawers and folders

Each button on the SmartCenter bar is called a *drawer*. To open a drawer, follow these steps:

1. Click the drawer containing the application, file, or feature that you want to open.

2. Click the folder tab that you want (if applicable).

3. Double-click the file or application that you want to open.

If you can't see all the SmartCenter buttons on-screen at one time, two scroll arrows appear at the right end of the bar. Click the right-arrow button to display additional buttons; then click the left-arrow button to display the first set of buttons.

To close an open SmartSuite drawer, click the Close button (the X) at the right end of the drawer. The following figure shows SmartCenter with the SmartSuite and Calendar drawers open.

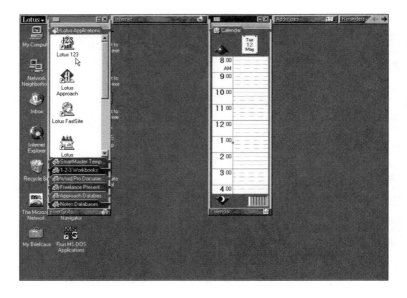

Need to plan a trip? If you have Internet access, you can book a flight or research accommodations directly from SmartCenter. Click the Travel Reservations folder in the Internet drawer of SmartCenter. Use the Maps folder in the Addresses drawer to locate interactive maps of locations anywhere in the United States and many other countries.

Customizing SmartCenter

You use the SmartCenter Properties dialog box to set preferences for SmartCenter. To access the SmartCenter Properties dialog box, follow these steps:

1. Click the Lotus button (the SmartCenter main menu) at the left end of the SmartCenter bar and select SmartCenter Properties.

2. From the SmartCenter Properties dialog box, edit the display options, sound effects, drawer front appearance, and other options by selecting the options that you want and then clicking OK to close the dialog box.

To add a drawer to SmartCenter, click the Lotus button at the left end of the SmartCenter bar and choose New Drawer. Type a label for the drawer, choose a drawer handle icon, and click OK.

To change properties for specific drawers or folders, right-click the drawer button and choose the option that you want from the shortcut menu. From the shortcut menu, you can change the properties of the drawer or folder, maximize the drawer so that it fills the screen, create a new folder, or delete the drawer.

If you want to remove SmartCenter from your screen, click the Lotus button at the left end of the SmartCenter bar and choose Exit SmartCenter.

SmartIcons

SmartIcons are those pretty on-screen buttons that provide quick access to common commands and actions. The SmartIcons appear just below the menu bar in all SmartSuite applications. SmartIcons are context-sensitive — a fancy term that simply means they change depending on what you're doing in an application. If you're creating a chart in 1-2-3, for example, the Chart SmartIcon bar appears. A SmartIcon bar is a group of related SmartIcons. At the left end of each SmartIcon bar is a blue bar with a downward-pointing triangle. Click the triangle to see a menu of available commands. You can add SmartIcons to existing bars or create your own SmartIcon bars that contain the SmartIcons you use most often.

Editing SmartIcon bars

You may occasionally need to add SmartIcons to a SmartIcon bar or remove SmartIcons that you don't use. You also can rearrange the SmartIcons. Follow these steps to change the icons that appear in a SmartIcon bar:

1. Select File⇨User Setup⇨SmartIcons Setup (or right-click a SmartIcon and choose SmartIcons Setup). The SmartIcons Setup dialog box appears.

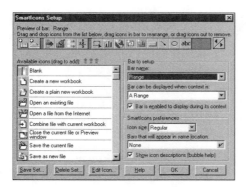

2. In the Bar Name drop-down list, select the name of the SmartIcon bar that you want to modify. The SmartIcon bar that you select appears at the top of the dialog box.

3. Choose one or more of the following actions:

- To add an icon to the SmartIcon bar, scroll through the Available Icons list until you find the icon that you want to add. Then click and drag the icon to any location in the SmartIcon bar at the top of the dialog box.

- To remove icons from the SmartIcon bar, drag them off the bar at the top of the dialog box.

- To rearrange icons on the SmartIcon bar, drag the icons to their new locations in the bar at the top of the dialog box.

4. Click the Save Set button to save your changes, and then click OK to close the dialog box.

Using SmartIcons

If you're not sure what a particular SmartIcon does, point to the SmartIcon and pause — a brief description of the SmartIcon appears inside a bubble. (Lotus refers to this as *bubble help.*) To use a SmartIcon, just click it. Depending on the SmartIcon's purpose, you may want to select data before clicking the SmartIcon.

You can hide or display SmartIcon bars as necessary. To change the SmartIcon bar that appears on-screen, try these techniques:

✦ Right-click anywhere within a SmartIcon bar and choose the name of the SmartIcon bar (such as Editing) from the bottom portion of the shortcut menu that appears. In the shortcut menu, a check mark appears next to names for SmartIcon bars that are currently open.

✦ To hide a SmartIcon bar from your screen, right-click a SmartIcon. From the shortcut menu, choose the name of the SmartIcon bar that you want to hide.

You can move a SmartIcon bar to another edge of the screen or inside the work area of an application (so that it "floats" over your data). Point to the blue bar that appears at the left end of a SmartIcon bar; the mouse pointer changes to an open hand. Then click and drag the SmartIcon bar to another side of the screen or inside the work area. The mouse pointer changes to a closed hand as you drag the SmartIcon bar. Release the mouse button to drop the SmartIcon bar in its new location.

Did your SmartIcons disappear from the screen? Don't worry. Choose View➪Show SmartIcons to redisplay them. If you want to hide your SmartIcons, choose View➪Hide SmartIcons. This command on the View menu changes depending on whether the SmartIcons are currently displayed. (In Word Pro, the command is worded a bit differently. Choose View➪Show/Hide➪SmartIcons to toggle the display of SmartIcons.)

Starting a Program

All SmartSuite applications run within the Windows operating system. To start a SmartSuite application, follow these steps:

1. Click the Start button in the Windows taskbar.

2. Select Programs➪Lotus SmartSuite.

3. Click the name of the application that you want to open.

You may prefer to open your SmartSuite applications from Lotus SmartCenter, the bar that appears at the top of your screen. To do so, click the button (or *drawer*) containing the application that you want to open, click the folder tab that you want, and then double-click the application's icon.

See also "SmartCenter," earlier in this part.

SuiteStart

SuiteStart is a group of icons that enable you to start SmartSuite applications with a single click. These icons appear on the taskbar in an area sometimes called the *tray*, at the opposite end from the Start button. You may see additional icons in this area, depending on your computer's setup. Point to a SuiteStart icon and pause to see a program name or description. Click the icon to start the application.

If you don't see the SuiteStart icons on your taskbar, choose Start➪Programs➪Lotus SmartSuite➪Lotus Accessories➪ SuiteStart.

To remove a single SuiteStart icon from the taskbar, right-click the icon and select the Remove Icon option. If you want to remove *all* the SuiteStart icons from your taskbar, right-click any of the SuiteStart icons and choose Exit.

Undo and Redo

Did you accidentally overwrite cell contents or a portion of a document? Maybe you pressed the wrong key and ended up with really strange stuff on your screen, or you moved data to the wrong location. Fear not — you may have an easy way out! SmartSuite provides the Undo feature, which enables you to reverse the last command or action performed in an application and return the file to its previous state.

Any of the following actions reverses the last action that you performed in an application:

➤ Click the Undo Last Command or Action SmartIcon.

➤ Choose Edit➪Undo.

➤ Press Ctrl+Z.

Some actions, such as those related to file operations like saving and closing files, can't be reversed. If your most recent command or action can't be undone, the Undo option appears dimmed on the Edit menu.

In Lotus Word Pro (but not the other SmartSuite programs), you also have the option of restoring actions or editing changes that you make with Undo. To perform a Redo in Word Pro, follow these steps:

1. Choose Edit➪Undo/Redo Special.

2. In the Edits You Can Redo box, select the actions that you want to redo and click Redo. Notice that the most recent actions appear at the top of the list box. To redo multiple actions, click the lowest action that you want to redo in the list; all actions appearing above that action are also redone.

3. Click OK.

Window Displays

Initially, each application shows one window with the current file (or a blank file) on-screen. As you begin working with multiple files on-screen at one time, however, your screen may become cluttered.

This section shows you how to change the look of your windows, close windows, and change the size of your windows. You also find out how to get windows out of your way without closing them. You may find other window "treatments" available in the individual applications. In 1-2-3, for example, you can split a single worksheet into two windows, allowing you to view different portions of the worksheet on-screen at the same time.

See also "Worksheet Views," in Part III.

If you have multiple windows open in an application, you can use the Window menu to quickly switch among them. Choose Window and then select the name of the window that you want to display from the bottom of the Window menu.

Arranging windows

Most SmartSuite applications enable you to tile or cascade your windows. Tiling windows displays them like floor tiles — blocks of windows that appear side-by-side or top to bottom. In most applications (with the exception of Freelance Graphics), you can tile windows either horizontally or vertically. When you cascade windows, the windows appear diagonally with their title bars showing — you see the contents of only the top cascaded window.

To arrange your open windows side-by-side, select Window⇨ Tile Left-Right (in Freelance Graphics, select Window⇨Tile). To arrange the windows from top to bottom, select Window⇨Tile Top-Bottom. If you want to cascade your windows to display them diagonally, choose Window⇨Cascade.

Closing windows

If you're finished with a window that appears on-screen, you can easily close the window to get it out of your way. (If you're not done using the window but it's taking up too much space, you can minimize the window — see the next section.)

To close a window, click the Close button (the X) that appears at the right end of the window's title bar. To redisplay data from a closed window, you need to open the file containing that data again.

Minimizing, maximizing, and restoring windows

To improve your on-screen visibility when you have several windows open at the same time (or just one open), you can minimize, maximize, or restore the windows. The following list describes your options:

✦ Click the Maximize button (which has one large window on it) to maximize a window so that it fills the entire work area. The Maximize button appears to the left of the window's Close button. When you maximize one window, you maximize all other open windows in that application, too (but, of course, you see only the one that you maximize).

✦ Click the Minimize button (which has a short, flat line on it) to minimize a window and store it temporarily as a button at the bottom of the application's work area. The Minimize button appears to the left of the Maximize or Restore button.

✦ Click the Restore button (which has two overlapping windows on it) to restore the window to its previous size after the window has been maximized or minimized. All other open windows are restored at the same time. When a window is in a restored state, you can move the window to another area of the screen by dragging the window's title bar.

Notice that the application's title bar also includes a Minimize button, a Maximize or Restore button, and a Close button. You can follow the same procedures described here to work with the application window.

Sizing windows

You can easily size windows manually to make them the exact size that you want. This procedure works only with restored windows — not with windows that are maximized or minimized (refer to the preceding section).

To manually size a window, move your mouse pointer to an edge or corner of the window; the pointer changes to a two-headed arrow. Then drag the edge or corner to resize the window. If you drag a corner of the window, you can change the height and width of the window in one step.

Part III

Lotus 1-2-3

Lotus 1-2-3 is the immensely popular spreadsheet component of Lotus SmartSuite Millennium Edition. This reliable number cruncher has been around almost as long as the first personal computers! The latest incarnation of 1-2-3 includes many more features than you'll probably ever need. This part covers the basics of 1-2-3 Millennium Edition, as well as some other useful features. After flipping through the sections in this part, you'll discover that using this spreadsheet is as easy as . . . (well, *you know!*). If you need more information on 1-2-3, you can find it in *Lotus 1-2-3 Millennium Edition For Dummies* by John Walkenbach (published by IDG Books Worldwide, Inc.).

In this part . . .

- ✔ **Creating charts**
- ✔ **Entering and editing text**
- ✔ **Formatting cells**
- ✔ **Using formulas and functions**
- ✔ **Selecting and navigating in the worksheet**
- ✔ **Changing your view of the worksheet**

Aligning Data

When you enter data in a cell, 1-2-3 automatically places text on the left side of a cell and numbers on the right side of a cell. If you want to change the alignment, 1-2-3 can do this for you in a snap! If your worksheet has several columns of numerical data, for example, your column headings may look better centered or right-aligned over the numbers rather than left-aligned.

You use the Alignment tab of the Range Properties InfoBox to change the alignment options. 1-2-3 gives you lots of choices for aligning data in cells. In addition to horizontal and vertical alignment, you can center data across multiple columns, wrap text in a cell, and rotate text. *See also* "InfoBoxes" in Part II.

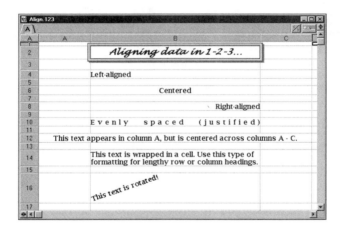

Aligning data horizontally in a cell

When you modify the alignment of data in a cell, you most often change the horizontal alignment. The quickest method of doing so is to use the Alignment button on the status bar. Follow these steps to change the horizontal alignment of data:

1. Select the cell or range containing the data you want to align.

2. Click the Alignment button on the status bar. A pop-up list of alignment buttons appears.

3. Click the button depicting the type of horizontal alignment that you want:

Button	What it Does
≡≡	Left-aligns text and right-aligns numbers (this is the standard alignment used in 1-2-3)
■	Left-aligns text and numbers
≣	Centers text and numbers
≣	Right-aligns text and numbers
▦	Evenly spaces text (but not numbers) across a cell; similar to justification in a word processor

Aligning data vertically in a cell

When you enter data in a cell, the data is automatically placed near the bottom of the cell. You can change the vertical alignment of cell data so that it appears at the top edge of a cell or centered vertically within the cell. If you want to place a border around a cell, you should center the text vertically within the cell. (See cell B2 in the preceding figure for an example of this.) Use these steps to change the vertical alignment of data in a cell:

1. Select the cell or range containing the data you want to align.

2. Choose Range⇨Range Properties to display the Range Properties InfoBox.

3. Click the Alignment tab of the InfoBox.

4. Click the button that corresponds to the vertical alignment you want — bottom, center, or top.

See also "Adding borders," later in this part.

Centering data across multiple cells

If your worksheet includes a title, you may want to center the title over the worksheet data. This option also works great if you want a column heading in your worksheet to appear centered over two or more columns of data. To center data across multiple cells, follow these steps:

1. Enter the data in the leftmost cell of the range in which you want to center the data.

2. Select the cells across which you want the text to be centered.

3. Choose Range⇨Range Properties to display the Range Properties InfoBox.

4. Click the Alignment tab of the InfoBox.

5. Click the button that corresponds to center alignment and then place a check mark in the Align Across Columns check box.

Rotating data in a cell

In 1-2-3, you can rotate data so that the characters are stacked (reading top to bottom), sideways, or rotated at an angle that you specify. Use rotated text when you need to include vertical titles for reports, or to label the sides of charts or tables. You can change the direction in which data appears in a cell by using the Orientation option in the Range Properties InfoBox. Follow these steps to rotate data in a cell:

1. Select the cell or range containing the data you want to rotate.

2. Choose Range⇨Range Properties to display the Range Properties InfoBox.

3. Click the Alignment tab of the InfoBox.

4. Select the rotation you want from the Orientation drop-down list. If you want to specify an angle for the rotation, select the last option in the Orientation drop-down list; then type the angle you want to use in the Angle text box.

If you can't get this feature to work, make sure that the Fit Largest Font option is selected on the Basics tab of the Range Properties InfoBox.

Wrapping text in a cell

If you want to display long text labels in a cell but don't want to change your column width, you can wrap the text within the cell. When you wrap text in a cell, 1-2-3 increases the row height until you see the entire text label. You can wrap only text in a cell — you can't wrap numbers. Use these steps to wrap text in a cell:

1. Select the cell or range containing the text you want to wrap.

2. Choose Range⇨Range Properties to display the Range Properties InfoBox.

3. Click the Alignment tab of the InfoBox.

4. Place a check mark in the Wrap Text In Cell check box.

Instead of breaking up lengthy column headings into multiple cells above a column of data, wrap the text of the entire column heading in a single cell. Then center the text within the wrapped cell for a neater appearance.

See also "Sizing Columns and Rows," later in this part.

Cell Comments

Do you occasionally need to comment on the data in specific cells in your worksheet, but you don't want to add explanatory text to the worksheet itself? If so, you'll like the cell comments feature in 1-2-3. With cell comments, you can annotate sales quotas that have been exceeded, or just simply add notes about your assumptions or source data. When you add a comment to a cell, 1-2-3 places a red dot in the top-left corner of the cell. That's how others who view your worksheets know to look for your comments.

Adding a comment to a cell

Follow these steps to add a comment to a cell:

1. Right-click the cell you want to add a comment to.

2. Choose Cell Comment from the shortcut menu.

3. Type the text for the comment in the Cell Comment text box.

4. If you want your name and the date of your comment to appear above the comment text, click the Name And Date Stamp button.

The following figure shows an example of a comment added to cell G10.

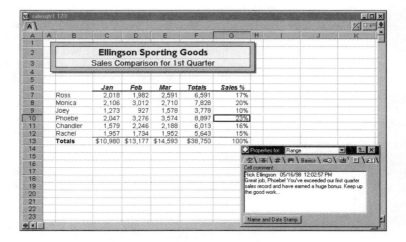

Editing and deleting cell comments

After you add a comment to your cell, you can easily edit the comment text or delete the comment if you no longer need it. Use these steps:

1. Right-click the cell with the comment. (Look for the red dot!)

2. Choose Cell Comment from the shortcut menu.

3. Edit the text as it appears in the Cell Comment text box. If you want to delete the comment, highlight the entire text of the comment and press Delete.

Viewing cell comments

If you see a red dot in the upper-left corner of a cell, this indicates that a comment has been added to the cell. To view a comment attached to a cell, follow these steps:

1. Right-click a cell that has a red dot in the corner.

2. Choose Cell Comment from the shortcut menu.

3. View the comment that appears in the Cell Comment text box of the Range Properties InfoBox.

Charts

The saying "a picture is worth a thousand words" certainly fits when referring to 1-2-3 charts. Charts enable you to illustrate the data in your worksheet, making the comparisons among numbers much easier to see and understand. Lotus 1-2-3 offers a multitude of charting capabilities, but you don't need to understand all the intricacies of charting to create a basic chart. This section explains how to switch to a different chart type and how to create and edit a chart.

Chart types

Lotus 1-2-3 provides many different chart types, including bar, pie, line, and area. When you first create a chart, 1-2-3 uses the bar chart type. Depending on the type of data that you're charting and the message that you want to convey, you may prefer to use a different chart type. For example, you can use a pie chart for a single data range to show the relationship of the parts to the whole and to each other, or you can use a line chart to illustrate linear changes in one or more sets of values. You can change the chart type as often as you like.

To switch to a different chart type, follow these steps:

1. Click the chart's frame to select the chart. Black handles surround the chart.

You must select a chart to gain access to the Chart menu. When changing the chart type, be sure to select the chart frame — not an object inside the chart.

2. Choose Chart⇨Chart Type to display the Chart Properties InfoBox.

3. Click the Type tab and select a new chart type from the list box. Your chart in the worksheet immediately changes to reflect your selections in the InfoBox.

When you select a chart, the Chart SmartIcon bar appears. You can click one of the SmartIcons depicting a chart type to switch to that style.

Creating a chart

A 1-2-3 chart is based on information that you've already entered in the worksheet. You should select the range containing the data you want to chart before you create the chart. When you're ready to create a chart, follow these steps:

1. Select the worksheet range containing the data you want to chart. Include data labels and a chart title in your selection if you want these to appear in the chart. Data labels normally consist of column and row headings, which 1-2-3 uses to create axis labels and the legend. If you place additional labels above the chart data, 1-2-3 uses this text to add titles to the chart.

2. Choose Create⇨Chart or click the Create a Chart SmartIcon. The mouse pointer changes to the shape of a miniature chart.

3. Click in the area of the worksheet where you want the top-left corner of the chart to appear (or click and drag in the worksheet to specify your own chart size). The chart is displayed in your worksheet.

To copy a chart, hold down the Ctrl key and drag an edge of the chart (not a chart handle) away from the selected chart. To move a chart, drag an edge of the chart and drop it in the desired location. If you want to resize a chart, select the chart and drag one of the black handles. You can delete a chart by selecting the chart and pressing the Delete key.

Editing a chart

After you create a chart, you may want to change the appearance of the chart by modifying chart properties such as the chart titles, series, legend, axes, plot area, colors, and layout. Follow these steps to modify the chart's appearance:

1. Click the chart to select it.

2. Open the Chart menu and select the option pertaining to the portion of the chart you want to modify.

3. A Chart Properties InfoBox appears. Select the appropriate InfoBox tab and make your desired selections.

Copying and Moving

You can copy or move cell data to other parts of the worksheet. This is a real time-saver because it saves you from having to retype existing data. The data that you move or copy is called the *source* data, and the new location for the data is called the *destination*. When you copy data, you create a duplicate copy of the data — the original data remains unchanged. Moving relocates the data to a destination that you choose. By default, 1-2-3 copies or moves the cell formatting and the cell contents.

Be careful when choosing the destination for a move or copy. Lotus 1-2-3 doesn't always warn you if you're about to overwrite existing worksheet data. If this happens, you can click the Undo Last Command or Action SmartIcon to reverse the move or copy operation.

See also "Copying and Pasting with the Clipboard" in Part VIII.

Copying data

Following are the basic steps for copying data to another location:

1. Select the source cell or range containing the data you want to copy.

2. Choose Edit⇨Copy or click the Copy to Clipboard SmartIcon.

3. Select the destination cell or the upper-left corner of the range to which you want to copy the data.

4. Choose Edit⇨Paste or click the Paste Clipboard Contents SmartIcon.

If you're copying data to a single destination that's close to the source range, you can quickly copy the data by dragging it. Select the source cell or range and point to an edge of the selection. Press and hold down the Ctrl key and then drag the selection to the destination. Release the mouse button and then release the Ctrl key.

If you want to copy data to a destination range that's adjacent to the source range, select both the source and destination ranges before the copy operation. Then choose either Edit⇨Copy Down or Edit⇨Copy Right, as appropriate.

See also "Using SmartFill," later in this part.

Moving data

Use the following procedure to move data from one location in the worksheet to another:

1. Select the source cell or range containing the data you want to move.

2. Choose Edit⇨Cut or click the Cut to Clipboard SmartIcon. The source data is removed from the worksheet.

3. Select the destination cell or the upper-left corner of the range to which you want to move the data.

4. Choose Edit⇨Paste or click the Paste Clipboard Contents SmartIcon.

If you're moving data to a single destination that's near the source range, you can drag the data to quickly move it. Select the source cell or range and point to an edge of the selection. Drag the selection to the destination.

Using Paste Special

The Paste Special dialog box lets you specify which properties of a selection are copied or moved to the destination. For example, you can copy the column widths and row heights to another range with or without copying cell contents. Follow these steps:

1. Select the source cell or range and choose Edit⇨Copy.

2. Select the destination cell or range and choose Edit⇨ Paste Special. The Paste Special dialog box appears.

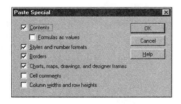

By default, 1-2-3 pastes the cell contents, styles, number formats, borders, and charts. You can deselect any of these options. You also can select to paste cell comments and the column widths and row heights.

3. Select the options you want and click OK.

Deleting

Lotus 1-2-3 makes it easy for you to delete cell contents, entire columns or rows, and entire worksheets that you no longer need. If you accidentally delete data, you can usually click the Undo Last Action or Command SmartIcon to retrieve the missing data.

See also "Editing and deleting cell comments," earlier in this part, and "Deleting a File" in Part II.

Deleting cell contents

To quickly delete cell contents, just select a cell or range and press the Delete key. You can use the Clear dialog box to selectively delete the contents, styles, number formats, borders, designer frames, cell comments, and scripts associated with a cell or range. Follow these steps to use the Clear dialog box:

1. Select the cell or range containing the data you want to delete.

2. Choose Edit⇨Clear. The Clear dialog box appears.

3. Select the options representing the properties you want to delete and click OK.

To quickly delete only the styles from a selected cell or range and not the cell contents, select the range and choose Edit⇨ Clear Styles.

Deleting entire columns or rows

If you delete a row or column in the worksheet, you delete all the data in the entire row or column, including data that may not be visible on-screen. Make sure that you check for possible data loss before you delete any columns or rows in your worksheets. Follow these steps to delete columns or rows:

1. Select at least one cell in each of the columns or rows you want to delete. (You also can click the row numbers or column letters in the worksheet frame to select entire rows or columns.)

2. Choose Range⇨Delete. The Delete dialog box appears.

3. Select either Rows or Columns and then click OK.

If you've grouped sheets together, deleting rows or columns in one sheet in the group will also delete the same rows or columns in all other sheets in the group. If you don't want this to happen, be sure to choose Sheet⇨Clear Sheet Group before performing this procedure.

See also "Selecting columns and rows," later in this part.

Deleting worksheets

You can delete a worksheet if you no longer need it in a workbook. Use either of the following methods:

✦ Select the sheet tab for each worksheet you want to delete and choose Sheet⇨Delete Sheet.

✦ Right-click the sheet tab and choose Delete Sheet.

Deleted worksheets are removed from the workbook immediately; 1-2-3 doesn't ask for confirmation before the deletion. Click the Undo Last Command or Action SmartIcon if you delete a worksheet in error.

If the Delete Sheet option appears dimmed, you have only one worksheet in the workbook. You can't delete all the sheets in a workbook.

See also "Selecting worksheets" and "Inserting worksheets," later in this part.

Editing Data

After you enter data in the worksheet, you may want to change the data. You can either type a new entry in the cell to replace the previous entry, or edit the existing entry. If you edit the data, you can do so either directly in the cell or in the contents box. Use the normal editing keys — arrow keys, Backspace, and Delete — to edit the cell.

See also "Entering Data," later in this part.

Editing in a cell

Follow these steps to edit data within a cell:

1. Double-click the cell containing the text you want to edit.

2. Edit the entry and press Enter.

Editing in the Contents box

To edit a cell entry by using the Contents box, follow these steps:

1. Select the cell containing the text you want to edit.

2. Click the Contents box in the Edit line.

3. Edit the entry and then click the Confirm button (the green check mark) or press Enter to accept the changes.

Finding and replacing data

You can search through a worksheet to find and replace characters in labels or values. 1-2-3 can search a selected range, the current worksheet, the current workbook, or all open workbooks.

You can find and replace values or labels.

Use the following steps to find data in a worksheet:

1. Choose Edit⇔Find & Replace. The Find and Replace dialog box appears.

2. In the Find text box, type the characters you want to search for.

3. Select the desired options in the Include and Match sections of the dialog box.

4. Click the Find button. Lotus 1-2-3 moves the cell pointer to the first occurrence.

5. Click the Find button again to find the next occurrence, or click Done if you're finished with the search operation.

Follow these steps to find and replace data in a worksheet:

1. Choose Edit⇔Find & Replace. The Find and Replace dialog box appears.

2. In the Find text box, type the characters you want to search for. Then type the new characters in the Replace With text box.

3. Select the desired options in the Include and Match sections of the dialog box.

4. Click the Find button. Lotus 1-2-3 moves the cell pointer to the first occurrence.

5. Click the Replace button to replace the characters and move to the next occurrence; or click Replace All to replace all occurrences.

6. Click Done when you're finished.

To correct misspelled words in your worksheet, choose Edit⇔Check Spelling; then click the Start button in the Check Spelling dialog box. Lotus 1-2-3 checks all cell entries, charts, and text blocks.

Entering Data

How do you build a worksheet? You enter data into it, of course!
Entering data in a 1-2-3 worksheet is as simple as selecting a cell,
typing the data, and pressing Enter. If you want to cancel an entry
as you type it, press Esc. Each cell can hold up to 512 characters.
You can enter any of the following types of data in a cell:

+ Numbers (also called *values*), including dates and times

+ Text (also called *labels*)

+ Formulas

If you enter data in a cell that already contains data, the new data
replaces the old data. You also can enter data in a cell by clicking
the Contents box (the gray box below the Help menu item), typing
the data, and clicking the Confirm button (the green check mark).
You can also press Enter instead of clicking the Confirm button. To
cancel an entry, click the Cancel button (the red X) or press Esc.

Instead of pressing Enter to confirm a cell entry, you can press any
of the arrow keys. This action enters the data in a cell and moves
the cell pointer to the next cell in the direction of the arrow key
that you press. This feature enables you to enter data down a
column (or across a row) much more quickly.

See also "Selecting cells and ranges" and "Moving Around the
Worksheet," later in this part.

Entering dates and times

Lotus 1-2-3 recognizes some, but not all, date and time formats
that you enter in a cell. To ensure that 1-2-3 recognizes your entry
as a date value, enter the date in the format mm/dd/yy (or mm/dd/
yyyy). If you omit the year number, 1-2-3 may assume that your
entry represents a fraction or a division operation. You can then
format the date to display it using any date format you want, such
as Nov-98, 06-Nov, 11/06/98, or 06-Nov-98. Times can be entered by
using the format hh:mm or hh:mm:ss. You can then format the cell
to display a different time format.

To enter a date or time in a cell, follow these steps:

1. Click the cell in which you want to enter a date or time.

2. Type the date or time number (such as **11/06/98** or **12:34**) and
then press Enter.

Lotus 1-2-3 Millennium Edition is Year 2000 compliant. This means that you can enter dates by using either two-digit (10/20/05) or four-digit (10/20/2005) date formats. For more information, choose Help⇨Year 2000.

See also "Number formatting," later in this part.

Entering numbers

Numbers (or *values*) include numeric characters as well as formulas and functions. Lotus 1-2-3 considers a cell entry to be a value if the first character that you type is a number. Any entry that combines letters with numbers is considered to be a label (as explained in the "Entering text" section).

To enter a number in a cell, follow these steps:

1. Click the cell in which you want to enter a number.

2. Type the number and then press Enter.

If you want to enter a number as a label (zip codes, phone numbers, or Item numbers, for example), you need to start your cell entry with a label-prefix character. Label-prefix characters tell 1-2-3 that you're entering a label; the characters also determine the cell's alignment. Choose from the following label prefixes:

Prefix	Effect
'	Left-aligns text
"	Right-aligns text
^	Centers text
\	Repeats text

To enter a number and simultaneously format it as currency or a percentage, type the currency symbol or percent sign when you enter the number (such as $150.23 or 75%). If you want the number to include decimal places, type those as well. This is sometimes faster than entering the number and then assigning a format to the number.

See also "Number formatting" and "Formulas," later in this part.

Entering text

Text entries (or *labels*) can include letters, numbers, or a combination of letters and numbers — a street address, for example. To enter a text entry in a cell, follow these steps:

1. Click the cell in which you want to enter text.

2. Type the text and then press Enter.

Text that you enter in a cell may appear to be truncated if the cell isn't wide enough and if the cell to the right of that cell contains data. Just widen the column to see all the data in the cell.

See also "Sizing Columns and Rows," later in this part.

Using SmartFill

The *SmartFill* feature automatically fills a range with a sequence of data, based on the data that is already entered in the range (such as numbers, dates, days of the week, and so on). To fill a range with data, follow these steps:

1. Select the cell or range containing the data on which you want to base the sequence.

2. Point to the bottom-right corner of the cell or range. The mouse pointer changes to display an arrow with four green triangles.

3. Click and drag to select the range you want to fill, and then release the mouse button.

Create your own custom SmartFill lists with data that you frequently enter in your worksheets, such as department names or divisions. After you create the list, you need to enter only one of the names in the list, and SmartFill fills in the rest of the names for you. Choose File➪User Setup➪SmartFill Setup and click the Help button in the dialog box for more information.

Formatting Data

Need to spice up that dull worksheet? You may want to use 1-2-3's formatting features to improve the appearance and effectiveness of the worksheet, making the data more readable and attractive. You can do so by changing the fonts, applying attributes such as bold and italics, adding borders and designer frames, and changing font or background colors.

You may also want to format the numbers in a worksheet so that readers know what type of information the numbers represent (such as currency, percentages, or dates). Most of these formatting changes can be made quickly via the status bar; others can be accessed through the Range Properties InfoBox. If your worksheet is set up in a certain way, you can use the Style Gallery to apply a number of formatting attributes and styles at one time.

Adding borders

You can add borders to your worksheet to emphasize important data. Borders can surround all sides of a cell or range, or they can be added to one or more sides. You can change the line style and color of borders and apply a designer frame.

Follow these steps to add a border:

1. Select the cell or range to which you want to add a border.

2. Choose Range⇨Range Properties to display the Range Properties InfoBox.

3. Click the Color, Pattern, and Line Style tab of the InfoBox.

4. In the Border area, click the button representing the border style you want to apply.

5. Select a line style and line color for the border. You must choose a line style; the default line color is Black, unless you change it.

6. If you want to use a fancy designer frame, place a check mark in the Designer Frame check box. Then choose the Frame Style and Frame Color you want to use.

 You can add an arrow to your worksheet to point to data in specific cells. Click the Draw a Forward-Pointing Arrow SmartIcon and then drag to the area of the worksheet in which you want the arrow to appear. To format the line, use the buttons on the status bar, or right-click the line and choose Drawing Properties. To reposition or resize the line, click the line and drag one of the black handles.

Applying background colors and patterns

Color can perform wonders when enhancing your worksheets. You can change the background color of ranges, charts, and other objects. In addition, you can change the color of text and numbers in your worksheets. (See the next section.) You also can add a textured pattern and a pattern color to the background.

Use the following steps to apply background colors and patterns to your worksheet:

1. Select the cell or range that you want to format.

2. Choose Range⇨Range Properties to display the Range Properties InfoBox.

3. Click the Color, Pattern, and Line Style tab of the InfoBox.

4. In the Interior section, select a background color, a pattern, and a pattern color.

Be careful when using background patterns. Some background patterns may make foreground text difficult to read or may print unpredictably. If you plan to print worksheet data that includes patterns, always test the patterns on your printer before you spend much time applying the formatting.

Applying bold, underline, or italics

Use the status bar to apply bold, underline, and italic attributes to a cell. Follow these steps:

1. Select the cell or range to which you want to apply bold, italics, or underline.

2. In the status bar, select one or more of the following buttons:

- Click the **B** button to apply boldface.
- Click the *I* button to apply italics.
- Click the U̲ button to apply underline.

3. If you want to remove any of these attributes, select the cell or range and click the appropriate button on the status bar to deselect it.

Changing fonts

You can change the font (text style) used in your worksheet, as well as the point size of the font and the font color. By default, 1-2-3 worksheets use the Arial 12-point font. Most font changes can be made by using the status bar.

Follow these steps to change the font, point size, and text color:

1. Select the cell or range containing the text you want to format.

2. Click one or more of the following buttons on the status bar and choose an option from the pop-up list that appears:

- Click the Font button (at the far left end of the status bar) to switch to a different font.

- Click the Point Size button (next to the Font button) to change the size of the chosen font.

- Click the Text Colors button (next to the Point Size button) to choose from a palette of colors.

If you need to access additional font attributes and point sizes, use the Text Format tab in the Range Properties InfoBox. The following figure shows you some of the options you have when using fonts to spruce up your worksheets. You may see different fonts on your system, depending on the software and printers that are installed.

Number formatting

By default, numbers that you enter in a worksheet initially appear in the General format. If you enter numbers by also typing currency symbols, commas, or percent signs, 1-2-3 automatically formats the numbers accordingly. Lotus 1-2-3 also recognizes certain date formats. You can always change the format of a number after you enter it in the worksheet.

To change the format of a number, follow these steps:

1. Select the cell or range containing the number(s) you want to format.

2. Click the Number Format button on the status bar and select the number format you want.

3. If you select a format that allows decimal places and you want to change the number of decimals displayed, click the Decimals button on the status bar and select the number of decimals you want displayed.

To see additional number format options, use the Number Format tab of the Range Properties InfoBox.

If asterisks (***) appear in a cell after you format a number, you must widen the column to display the number using your chosen format.

Using the Style Gallery

You can use the Style Gallery in 1-2-3 to quickly format a range of data with a preformatted template. Just follow these steps:

1. Select the range containing the data you want to format.

2. Choose Range➪Range Properties to display the Range Properties InfoBox.

3. Click the Named Style tab of the InfoBox.

4. Click the Style Gallery button. The Style Gallery dialog box appears.

5. In the Style Templates list, select the template you want to use; then click OK.

The following figure shows the Style Gallery dialog box with the Picture2 style template selected.

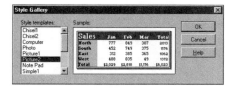

Formulas

One of the major strengths of 1-2-3 is the program's capability to calculate formulas. You can enter formulas that perform calculations on numbers and text in the worksheet. As with text entries, formulas can use up to 512 characters. When you select a cell containing a formula, the contents box displays the formula, and the worksheet cell displays the result of the formula. Examples of formulas include the following:

Formula	Meaning
+D7	Displays the contents of cell D7
+A2*A3	Multiplies the contents of cells A2 and A3
+(B10+B15)/C2	Adds the contents of cells B10 and B15 and divides that result by the contents of cell C2

Parentheses in a formula tell 1-2-3 the order to use when performing calculations. If you don't use parentheses in a formula, 1-2-3 performs exponentiation first, then multiplication and division, and finally addition and subtraction.

See also "Functions," later in this part.

Cell references

Cell addresses in a formula can be relative, absolute, or mixed. Lotus 1-2-3 normally uses relative references in a formula, unless you specify otherwise. When you copy a formula that contains *relative references*, 1-2-3 automatically adjusts the addresses to reflect their new location. You can use *absolute references* when you don't want the cell addresses in a formula to change, such as when you move a formula to a different part of the worksheet. Absolute references use a dollar sign preceding the sheet letter, column letter, and row number. In *mixed references*, part of the cell address is absolute, and the other part is relative.

Follow these steps to change the type of cell reference in a formula:

1. Double-click the cell containing the formula.

2. Move the cursor to the cell address in the formula that you want to edit.

3. Press F4 to cycle through the cell reference types. When you get to the reference type you want to use, press Enter to complete the formula.

Editing formulas

Editing a formula works the same way as editing any other cell entry. You can edit the formula two different ways: by double-clicking the cell or by clicking inside the contents box. Use the Backspace, Delete, and arrow keys to edit the formula, and press Enter when you're finished editing the formula.

If you're unsure of why 1-2-3 won't accept a formula that you try to enter in a cell, type an apostrophe at the beginning of the cell and press Enter. The program converts the formula to a label, but you can fix the formula and remove the label prefix when you find the error.

Entering formulas

You can enter formulas by typing them manually in the worksheet or by pointing to cells that you want a formula to compute. Formulas can consist of mathematical operators, cell references, range names, values, text, and parentheses. Use descriptive range names in a formula whenever possible to make it easier for you to remember the purpose of a formula. More complex formulas use function names, such as @AVG. The following table lists the operators you can use in formulas:

Operator	Description
+ (plus sign)	Addition
- (minus sign)	Subtraction
* (asterisk)	Multiplication
/ (slash)	Division
^ (caret)	Exponentiation

Follow these steps to enter a formula in a cell:

1. Select the cell in which you want to enter the formula, and then type a plus sign (+) to begin the formula.

2. Type or click the first cell reference in the formula (or type a value or range name).

3. Type a mathematical operator (see table above); then type or click the next cell reference.

4. Repeat the previous step until you complete the formula, and then press Enter.

If 1-2-3 displays asterisks (***) in the cell containing the formula, widen the column containing that cell to see the formula result.

See also "Naming Cells and Ranges," later in this part.

Linking worksheets

You can create formulas in 1-2-3 that link data across multiple worksheets or workbooks. This feature is particularly useful in consolidation applications — using one worksheet in a workbook to summarize data contained in the other worksheets, for example. To create this type of formula, specify the worksheet in which the data is located (indicated by a sheet letter or name), followed by a colon and the cell address. The following formula sums data from cell G15 across worksheets B, C, and D:

```
+B:G15+C:G15+D:G15
```

To use a formula that links data across workbooks, you must precede the cell reference with the file name enclosed in double-angle brackets, like this:

```
+<<Quarter1>>A:B7+<<Quarter2>>C:D10
```

The workbooks referenced in the formula do *not* need to be open in order for linking to work properly, but the files must reside in the default workbook folder. (To change or view the default workbook folder, choose File⇨User Setup⇨1-2-3 Preferences and click the File Locations tab.)

Functions

Lotus 1-2-3 provides hundreds of built-in formulas, called *functions*, to help you with more complex worksheet calculations. Unless you're an engineer (or a mad scientist!), you'll probably use only a dozen or so of these in your worksheets. When you enter a function in a cell, the result of the calculation appears in that cell, and the function itself appears in the contents box on the edit line. This section shows you how to enter functions and covers some of the functions that you'll probably find the most useful.

All 1-2-3 functions begin with the @ sign, followed by the name of the function, such as @SUM, @AVG, and @COUNT. Most functions also require you to enter one or more arguments — inputs that the function needs to perform the calculation — after the function name. These arguments must be separated by commas and enclosed within parentheses. To add the numbers contained in cells B2 through B10, for example, you would enter the function **@SUM(B2..B10)** in the cell that you want to display the function's result. (Use two periods to separate the first and last cells in a range that you want to add.) You also can use named ranges for the arguments in a function. In the preceding example, if you assign the name SALES to the range B2..B10, you can enter **@SUM(SALES)** in the cell.

See also "Formulas," covered earlier in this part, and "Naming Cells and Ranges," later in this part.

Entering functions

To enter a function, you can just type it in manually (using the correct syntax, of course!) and then press Enter. If you don't know the function name or the arguments that a function requires, follow these steps to use the @Function selector:

1. Click the @Function selector in the Edit line (that little button with the @ symbol and a down-pointing triangle).

2. In the drop-down list, if you see the function you want, click that function's name and then skip to Step 6. Otherwise, if you want a different function (or more information), click List All.

3. In the @Function List dialog box, choose a category from the Category drop-down list if you want to limit the display of functions in the @Functions list to a certain area of functions (such as Calendar or Logical).

4. Select the function you want from the @Functions list. A description of that function (along with the formula syntax) appears at the bottom of the dialog box.

5. After you select the function you want, click OK.

6. Lotus 1-2-3 places the function in the cell and highlights the placeholders for the function's arguments (if any). Supply the arguments for the function and press Enter when you're done.

Can't figure out how to supply the arguments for your function? Go back to the @Function List dialog box, select the function, and click the Help button. The program displays a Help window with lots of information on that specific function, along with several examples of how to use the function.

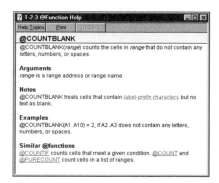

SmartLabels — words that 1-2-3 associates with certain formulas — can enter functions in the worksheet for you. If you type the word **Totals**, for example, 1-2-3 automatically supplies the @SUM formulas in appropriate cells beside or below the SmartLabel. Lotus 1-2-3 also provides other SmartLabels, such as Average and

Max, and you can set up your own as well. For more information, search on "SmartLabels" in 1-2-3's Help system.

Using common functions

The following table lists some of the most commonly used functions in 1-2-3, along with a description of each function's purpose.

Function	Description
@AVG	Calculates the average of a list of values.
@COUNT	Counts the number of nonblank cells in a range.
@IF	Displays one result if a test condition is true or another result if the condition evaluates to false.
@MAX	Finds the largest value in a range.
@MIN	Finds the smallest value in a range.
@NOW	Displays the current date and time.
@PMT	Calculates the periodic payment on a loan.
@ROUND	Rounds a value to a specific number of decimal places.
@SUM	Sums a range of values. You can use the Sum Values SmartIcon to quickly sum a range of values above or to the left of the current cell.
@TODAY	Displays the current date.

Inserting

Just as you can delete rows, columns, or worksheets, you also can insert them where you choose in a workbook. In addition, you can insert blank cells in a worksheet by shifting surrounding cells to make room for new cells.

Inserting cells

To insert blank cells in a worksheet, follow these steps:

1. Select the cells in which you want to insert new, blank cells.

2. Choose Range⇨Insert. The Insert dialog box appears.

3. Select the Insert In Selected Range Only check box.

4. To shift the selected range down, select Rows; to shift the selected range to the right, select Columns.

5. Click OK. The blank cells are inserted in the worksheet.

Inserting new columns or rows

You can insert entire columns or rows in the worksheet to make room for more data. When you insert columns or rows, existing columns move to the right, and existing rows move down. If you insert a new column or row within the borders or a range name, the range name expands to include the new columns or rows.

Use the following steps to insert new columns or rows:

1. Select at least one cell for each of the columns or rows, where you want to insert them. (You also can click the row numbers or column letters in the worksheet frame to select entire rows or columns.)

2. Choose Range⇨Insert. The Insert dialog box appears.

3. Select either Rows or Columns and click OK.

If you group sheets together, inserting rows or columns in one sheet in the group also inserts the same rows or columns in all other sheets in the group. If you don't want this to happen, be sure to choose Sheet⇨Clear Sheet Group before performing this procedure.

See also "Selecting columns and rows," later in this part.

Inserting worksheets

New 1-2-3 workbooks contain only a single worksheet. You can insert new, blank worksheets, placing them before or after the current sheet. You can insert up to 255 additional worksheets (256 total). Use either of the following methods:

✦ Click the New Sheet button to insert a blank worksheet after the current sheet. The New Sheet button is located at the opposite end of the sheet tabs.

✦ Choose Create⇨Sheet. Type the number of sheets you want to insert and choose to place them before or after the current sheet. Click OK.

See also "Selecting worksheets," later in this part, and "Deleting worksheets," earlier in this part.

Keyboard Shortcuts

Many tasks or operations in 1-2-3 can be performed by using either the keyboard or the mouse (or a combination of the two!). If you're entering data in a worksheet, it may be faster for you to keep your hands on the keyboard and press a key combination to execute a command. For example, instead of reaching for the mouse and clicking the Save SmartIcon, you can press Ctrl+S (hold down the Ctrl key and then tap the letter S) to save the current file.

Dozens of keyboard shortcuts are available in 1-2-3 — too many to list in this book, unfortunately. The following procedure shows how to access lists of the shortcut keys within 1-2-3's Help system:

1. Choose Help⇨Help Topics. The Help Topics dialog box appears.

2. Click the Contents tab and double-click the topic named Tools For Getting Your Work Done.

3. Double-click the Using The Keyboard topic.

4. In the resulting list, double-click the topic relating to the category of keyboard shortcuts that you want to see (such as Function Keys).

5. View or print the information in the Help window and then click the Close button to close the window when you're finished.

Moving Around the Worksheet

To enter data in a worksheet, you must first move to the cell that you want to contain the data. You can use either the keyboard or the mouse to navigate the worksheet.

See also "Entering Data," earlier in this part.

Navigating with the keyboard

The following table lists the most common keystrokes for moving around the worksheet:

Key	Action
→ or ←	Moves right or left one column
↑ or ↓	Moves up or down one row
PgDn	Moves down one worksheet screen

(continued)

(continued)

Key	Action
PgUp	Moves up one worksheet screen
Tab (or Ctrl+→)	Moves right one worksheet screen
Shift+Tab (or Ctrl+←)	Moves left one worksheet screen
Home	Moves to cell A1 in the current worksheet
Ctrl+Home	Moves to cell A:A1 in the current workbook
Ctrl+PgUp	Moves to the preceding worksheet in a workbook
Ctrl+PgDn	Moves to the following worksheet in a workbook
F5	Displays the Go To dialog box, in which you can type the cell address you want to move to

Navigating with the mouse

The following table lists the most common mouse movements for navigating the worksheet:

Navigation Action	Mouse Movement
Move directly to a cell	Click the cell
Move to a cell that's not visible	Use the scroll bars to scroll the worksheet; click the cell when it becomes visible
Move to a named range	Click the Navigator button and then click the range name from the drop-down list
Switch to another sheet in the workbook	Click the sheet tab

Naming Cells and Ranges

Naming a cell or range makes it easier for you to find, select, and use range names in formulas. Use letters, numbers, and spaces in range names; don't use special characters such as periods, commas, or asterisks.

Follow these steps to assign a name to a cell or range:

1. Select the cell or range you want to name.

2. Choose Range⇨Name. The Name dialog box appears.

3. In the Name text box, type a descriptive name for the range. You can type up to 15 characters.

4. If you want to name another range, click Add. Then use the Range text box to select another range, and type a name for the new range in the Name box.

5. When you're finished, click OK to close the dialog box.

After you assign a range name, you can quickly jump to that range (or use it in a formula) via the Navigator button. The Navigator button appears beside the selection indicator, in the Edit line. Click the Navigator button and then click the range name from the drop-down list.

Don't assign range names that can be mistaken for cell references, such as Q4 or CO2. Also avoid using function names, key names, and macro commands as range names. Otherwise, you may get unexpected results when using these range names in formulas.

Naming Worksheets

Naming worksheets with descriptive names helps you locate the worksheet you want to use. These names can be used in place of sheet letters in formulas, functions, or macros. You can assign names using up to 15 characters. As with named ranges, you should use only letters, numbers, and spaces in worksheet names. Follow these steps:

1. Double-click the tab of the sheet you want to name.

2. Type a new name for the sheet and then press Enter.

Printing

Once you finish creating your awe-inspiring worksheet, you'll most likely want to preview your work and then print a copy of it. You can print an entire workbook, the current worksheet, or any range or object that you select. You can use the default print settings to quickly print one copy of a worksheet, or you can use the InfoBox to customize the print and page settings.

See also "InfoBoxes" in Part II.

Previewing and changing the page setup

Always preview your work before you print. This saves you time (not to mention paper!), enabling you to make all necessary adjustments before you print. Use the following procedure to preview your work and make any setup changes that are necessary:

1. Select the worksheet range that you want to preview.

2. Choose File➪Preview & Page Setup or click the Print Preview SmartIcon.

Lotus 1-2-3 displays the current workbook in the left window and the Preview window on the right. The Preview & Page Setup Properties InfoBox also appears on-screen. Use this InfoBox to change margins and orientation, add headers and footers, specify pages to print, and lots more.

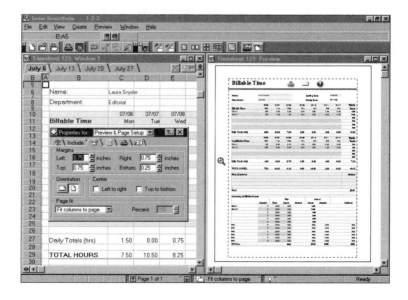

3. Change the desired options in the InfoBox until you're satisfied with the preview of the worksheet.

 4. Click the Close the Current File or Preview Window SmartIcon to return to the worksheet. (Refer to the "Printing a worksheet" section following this section for instructions on printing.)

 While in the Preview window, you can immediately print the worksheet by using the current print settings. To do so, click the Quick-print the Current Selection SmartIcon.

Printing a worksheet

When you're ready to print your worksheet data, follow these steps:

 1. Choose File➪Print or click the Print SmartIcon. The Print dialog box opens.

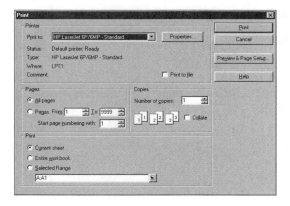

2. In the Printer area, select the printer you want to use. Your default printer should already be selected.

3. In the Print area, select what you want to print: Current Sheet, Entire Workbook, or Selected Range. If you choose Selected Range, type the page range in the text box or use the range selector to specify the page range in the worksheet. (If you preselected a range before you opened the Print dialog box, this range already appears in the Selected Range text box.)

4. In the Pages area, select the pages you want to print (or keep the default of All Pages).

5. In the Copies area, select the number of copies you want to print and click the Collate option if you want to collate the copies.

6. Click Print to begin printing.

TIP

Most often, you'll probably want to print a single copy of the current worksheet to the default printer. In that case, just click the Print SmartIcon and then click the Print button in the Print dialog box.

Selecting

In 1-2-3, you first select a worksheet or a portion of a worksheet before you enter data or perform a command. You can select any of the following: a cell, a range, a multiple-worksheet (3D) range, a collection (a group of non-adjacent cells or ranges), a column or row, or a sheet in the workbook. To cancel a selection, press Esc or click any cell in the worksheet.

Selected cell⌐ Selected range Selected column

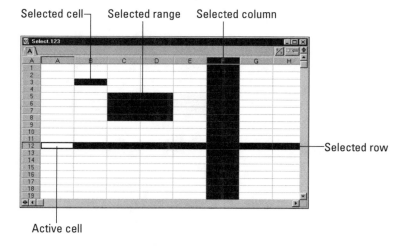

⌐Selected row

Active cell

Refer to the selection indicator (the gray box at the left end of the Edit line, below the main menu) to see the currently selected cell address, range address, or range name.

Selecting cells and ranges

To enter data in a cell or perform a command on a cell, you must first select the cell. To select a single cell, just click the cell. If you don't see the cell on-screen, move to that cell by using the keyboard or the mouse. You also can move to a specific cell by pressing F5, typing the cell address, and clicking OK.

Many commands in 1-2-3 act on ranges in the worksheet. To select a range, follow these steps:

1. Click a cell in any corner of the range.

2. Hold down the left mouse button and drag across cells to the opposite corner of the range.

3. The selected range is highlighted in the worksheet; release the mouse button.

If you need to select a large range that isn't entirely visible on-screen, click one corner of the range; then scroll to the opposite end of the range, hold down the Shift button, and click the opposite cell.

To select a 3D range across multiple worksheets, follow the preceding steps to select a range in the first worksheet. Then hold down the Shift key and click the sheet tab for the last sheet in the range.

See also "Moving Around the Worksheet," earlier in this part.

Selecting columns and rows

When you select a column or row, all the cells contained in that column or row are also selected — even those that aren't visible on-screen. Use the following techniques to select rows and columns:

✦ To select a single column, click the column letter. To select multiple adjacent columns, drag across the column letters. If you want to select multiple columns that aren't adjacent to each other, hold down the Ctrl key and click the column letters for each column you want to select.

✦ To select a single row, click the row number. To select multiple adjacent rows, drag across the row numbers. If you want to select multiple rows that aren't adjacent, hold down the Ctrl key and click the row numbers for each row you want to select.

Selecting worksheets

To make a worksheet active, just click the sheet tab. If you want to select all the cells in a worksheet, click the sheet letter (*not* the sheet tab) that appears just above the row numbers. Select any cell in the worksheet to cancel the selection. You can right-click a sheet tab and choose Sheet Properties to access the Sheet Properties InfoBox for a particular worksheet. If you want to change the properties of several worksheets at once, select the first sheet tab, click the tab again to activate the tab (the background of the tab turns white), hold down the Ctrl key, and then click the other sheet tabs you want to select. To select several adjacent sheet tabs, hold down the Shift key (instead of Ctrl) as you click the last tab.

If you want your workbook to contain several adjacent worksheets with similar formatting, you may want to group the sheets. When you group sheets, the styles and formatting that you apply to one sheet are automatically applied to all other sheets in the group. Use the Sheet⇨Group Sheets command to access this feature. When you're finished, remember to choose Sheet⇨Clear Sheet Group to cancel the group command.

To move a sheet tab, first point to any edge of the sheet tab so that the mouse pointer changes to a hand. Then drag the sheet tab and drop it in the new location. Use the same procedure to create a copy of a sheet, except hold down the Ctrl key before you drag the tab to a new location.

Sizing Columns and Rows

In a new 1-2-3 worksheet, all columns start with a width of 9 characters, and all rows start with a height of 14 points. As you begin building the worksheet, you may want to change the size of individual columns or rows.

Changing the column width

If a column is too narrow, values appear in Scientific format (such as $1.2E+010$) or as asterisks (***). Long text entries may appear to be truncated if the cell to the right contains data. To address these problems, just widen the column. Use either of these methods to change the width of a column:

+ Move the mouse pointer to the column border — to the right of the column letter you want to resize. When the pointer changes to a double-sided arrow, drag left or right to resize the column.

+ Right-click the column letter and choose Range Properties. Click the Basics tab in the InfoBox and make your desired selections in the Column area. (Notice that you also can hide columns and insert column page breaks from this tab of the InfoBox.)

To automatically size a column to fit the widest entry, double-click the column border to the right of the column letter.

Changing the row height

Lotus 1-2-3 automatically adjusts the row height to accommodate changes in point size for data in that row. However, you may occasionally want to change the height of a row to add more white space between rows and improve the worksheet's appearance. Use either of these methods to change the height of a row:

✦ Move the mouse pointer to the row border — below the row number you want to resize. When the pointer changes to a double-sided arrow, drag up or down to resize the row.

✦ Right-click the row number and choose <u>R</u>ange Properties. Click the Basics tab in the InfoBox and make your desired selections in the Row area. (Notice that you can also hide rows and insert row page breaks from this tab of the InfoBox.)

If you need to resize a row to fit the tallest entry, double-click the row border below that entry's row number.

SmartMaster Templates

SmartMasters are prebuilt templates that include data, formatting, macros, and formulas for a particular type of application, such as amortizing a loan, creating an invoice or personal budget, or generating a purchase order. These templates can give you a head start if you need to create a workbook based on these and other common tasks.

You can access the SmartMaster templates from the Welcome to 1-2-3 dialog box that appears when you start 1-2-3, or from the New Workbook dialog box. Follow these steps to use a SmartMaster template:

1. If you don't see the Welcome to 1-2-3 dialog box on-screen, choose <u>F</u>ile➪<u>N</u>ew Workbook (or click the Create a New Workbook SmartIcon).

2. Select the template you want to use from the <u>S</u>martMaster Templates list.

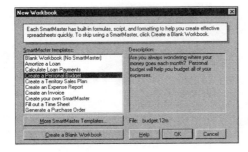

3. Click OK. The template you selected appears on-screen.

4. For information on how to use the SmartMaster, click the round question mark button that appears near the top of the worksheet.

Sorting Data

Lotus 1-2-3 enables you to sort your worksheet data in the order you specify, based on the contents of one or more columns in a range. You can sort data in ascending order (A to Z, 0 to 9) or descending order (Z to A, 9 to 0). Follow these steps to sort a range of data in the worksheet:

1. Select the range containing the data you want to sort.

2. Choose Range⇨Sort. The Sort dialog box appears.

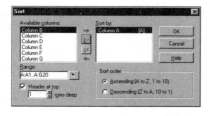

3. In the Available Columns list, select the column on which you want to sort and then click the >> button to move the selection to the Sort By list.

4. If you want to sort on additional columns, repeat Step 3.

5. In the Sort Order area, select either Ascending or Descending.

6. If your selected range includes a column header, select the Header At Top check box and specify the number of rows in your header.

7. Click OK to close the dialog box and perform the sort.

Worksheet Views

You can change the way that 1-2-3 displays worksheets in the worksheet window. This enables you to more easily compare data from two different worksheets or different areas of the same worksheet.

To access additional view options that affect what you see on-screen (such as gridlines, sheet tabs, and scroll bars), choose View➪Set View Preferences and click the View tab (if necessary). You can also choose File➪User Setup➪1-2-3 Preferences for more options.

See also "Window Displays" in Part II.

Freezing row or column titles

Most worksheets you create are probably large enough that they can't be displayed entirely on one screen. This can make your worksheet data difficult to read when your row or column headings scroll off the screen. Lotus 1-2-3 enables you to freeze the row and column titles so that they remain frozen on the screen as you scroll down or across the worksheet. Follow these steps:

1. Position the worksheet so that the titles you want to freeze on-screen appear at the top and left sides of the screen.

2. Select the cell that is just below the column headings and/or just to the right of the row headings.

3. Choose View➪Titles. The Titles dialog box appears.

4. Select one or both of the check boxes to indicate what you want to freeze: Rows Above Current Cell and/or Columns Left Of Current Cell.

5. Click OK to close the dialog box.

To unfreeze the titles and restore the worksheet to the normal display, choose View➪Titles and uncheck one or both of the check boxes.

Splitting panes

In 1-2-3, you can split the worksheet window into two horizontal or two vertical panes. You also can split the window into four rectangular panes. This technique is useful for large worksheets — you can see different parts of the same worksheet on-screen at once. To split the worksheet window into multiple panes, follow these steps:

1. Select the cell that's located where you want the window to be split. The position of the cell pointer determines the size of each pane.

2. Choose View➪Split. The Split dialog box appears.

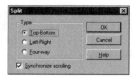

3. In the Type area of the dialog box, select the type of split you want to use: Top-Bottom, Left-Right, or Four-Way.

4. If you want the individual window panes to scroll separately, uncheck the Synchronize Scrolling check box.

5. Click OK to close the dialog box.

To remove the split panes and restore the worksheet window, choose View➪Clear Split.

Use the mouse to quickly split the worksheet window into panes. Drag the horizontal splitter (the button just above the vertical scroll bar) down to create horizontal panes. Drag the vertical splitter (the button just left of the horizontal scroll bar) to the right to create vertical panes. Drag the splitters to their original positions to restore the worksheet window.

Zooming the worksheet

You can specify a percentage (from 25% to 200%) by which to enlarge or shrink the worksheet display. Change the zoom to a larger percentage to enlarge the data. (Fewer cells are displayed.) To see a bird's eye view of your worksheet (smaller data, but more cells), use a smaller zoom percentage. Changing the zoom percentage has no effect on printing. Use one of these options:

✦ Choose View➪Zoom and select the percentage to switch to a specified zoom level.

✦ Choose View➪Zoom to Custom Level to switch the zoom back to the custom level (87%, by default).

To change the custom zoom level, choose View➪Set View Preferences and click the View tab. Then change the Custom Zoom % to the desired percentage and click OK.

Part IV

Word Pro

As you may have guessed, Word Pro is the word processing software provided with Lotus SmartSuite Millennium Edition. If you've never used a word processor before (or if you're switching to Word Pro from another word processor), you'll find that Word Pro makes it easy for you to create a document from scratch. You also can use Word Pro's custom SmartMaster templates to quickly create common documents like letters, memos, faxes, newsletters, and calendars. This part focuses on Word Pro tasks that you most likely use on a daily basis, such as creating, editing, formatting, and printing documents.

In this part...

- ✔ Creating documents based on templates
- ✔ Entering and editing text in your documents
- ✔ Formatting text and paragraphs
- ✔ Inserting special elements, such as tables, headers, and footers
- ✔ Proofing your documents
- ✔ Using the new ViaVoice feature to dictate text directly into a Word Pro document

Bulleted Lists

You can use bulleted lists in a document to help emphasize key points. Follow these steps to enter a bulleted list in your document:

1. Position the insertion point where you want to begin a bulleted list.

2. Click the Insert Default Bullet SmartIcon. A bullet appears in the document.

3. Type the text for the first bulleted item and then press Enter to begin the next bulleted item.

4. After typing the final bulleted item, press Enter and then click the Insert Default Bullet SmartIcon again to turn off the bullet formatting.

To insert new bullets in the middle of a bulleted list, position the insertion point at the end of a bulleted paragraph and press Enter. The bullet formatting carries to the new paragraph.

To skip a bullet within a bulleted list (while still keeping the text aligned with other bullets in the list), click the Skip Bullet/Number SmartIcon, type the text of the paragraph, and then press Enter. Click this SmartIcon again to resume the bulleted list.

To change the appearance or other properties of existing bullets, follow these steps:

1. Select the bulleted text and then choose Text⇨Text Properties (or press Alt+Enter) to display the Text Properties InfoBox.

2. Click the Bullet and Number tab in the InfoBox.

3. In the InfoBox, click the button representing the bullet style you want to use, and then select any other options you want to apply.

To apply bullets to (or remove bullets from) existing paragraphs of text, select the paragraphs and then click the Insert Default Bullet SmartIcon.

See also "Numbered Lists," later in this part.

Columns

If you create a newsletter, you may want to format your document to display text in multiple columns across the page. To add columns to your document, follow these steps:

1. Choose Page⇨Page Properties. The Page Properties InfoBox appears.

2. Click the Newspaper Columns tab in the InfoBox.

3. Specify the number of newspaper columns you want to use.

4. Select additional options that you want to apply, such as Space Between Columns, Line Style, Line Width, and Line Color.

5. If you want to balance the text between the columns, select the Column Balance check box.

To remove newspaper columns, display the Page Properties InfoBox, and type **1** in the Number of Newspaper Columns box.

Copying and Moving

You can copy or move existing text to other parts of the document. This saves time because you don't need to retype the text. By default, Word Pro copies or moves with the text any text formatting you've applied.

If you accidentally overwrite text during a copy or move procedure, remember that you can click the Undo Last Command or Action SmartIcon to reverse the move or copy operation.

See also "Selecting Text," later in this part, and "Copying and Pasting with the Clipboard" in Part VIII.

Copying text

Use the following steps to copy text to another location:

1. Select the text that you want to copy.

2. Choose Edit⇨Copy or click the Copy to Clipboard SmartIcon.

3. Position the insertion point where you want the copied text to appear.

4. Choose Edit⇨Paste or click the Paste Clipboard Contents SmartIcon.

If you copy text to a nearby location, you may prefer to copy the text by dragging it. Select the text you want to copy and then move the mouse pointer onto the selected text. The I-beam pointer displays a hand. Press and hold down the Ctrl key and then drag the selected text to the destination; a red vertical bar indicates where the copied text will appear. Release the mouse button and then release the Ctrl key.

Moving text

To move text from one location to another in a document, follow these steps:

1. Select the text that you want to move.

2. Choose Edit⇨Cut or click the Cut to Clipboard SmartIcon. The text is removed from the document.

3. Position the insertion point where you want the text to appear.

4. Choose Edit⇨Paste or click the Paste Clipboard Contents SmartIcon.

If you move text to a nearby location, you can drag the text to quickly move it. Select the text that you want to move and then move the mouse pointer onto the selected text. The I-beam pointer displays a hand. Drag the selected text to the destination; a red vertical bar indicates where the moved text will appear. Release the mouse button to drop the text in its new location.

Creating a New Document

To create a new Word Pro document, you can begin working with a blank document or use an existing SmartMaster template. *SmartMasters* give you a head start because they already include the text and formatting for common applications such as memos, labels, and faxes.

Creating a template-based document

You can access the SmartMaster templates from the Welcome to Lotus Word Pro dialog box that appears when you start Word Pro, or from the New Document dialog box. To use a SmartMaster template, follow these steps:

1. If you see the Welcome to Lotus Word Pro dialog box on-screen, click the Create a New Document From A SmartMaster tab. Then click the Browse for More Files button. The New Document dialog box appears.

If you don't see a dialog box, choose File⇨New Document (or click the Create a New Document SmartIcon). The New Document dialog box appears.

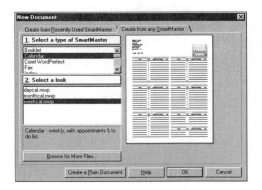

2. Click the Create From Any SmartMaster tab and then select the type of SmartMaster that you want to use from the Select A Type Of SmartMaster list box.

3. In the Select A Look list box, select a look for the template you selected. A preview of the selected template and look appears in the right half of the dialog box.

4. Click OK. (Depending on the type of SmartMaster you chose, you may see another dialog box requesting information needed for the SmartMaster. Enter the requested information and then click OK.) A new document based on the template you selected appears on-screen.

Opening a blank document

Most often, you'll probably want to create a new document from scratch — by starting with a blank document. Follow these steps:

1. Choose File⇨New Document (or click the Create a New Document SmartIcon). The New Document dialog box appears.

2. Click the Create A Plain Document button. A blank document appears on-screen.

Use the Open an Existing Document SmartIcon if you want to edit a document that you've already saved to disk.

Deleting Text

You can easily delete individual characters of text or blocks of text in a document. Use any of the following methods to delete text:

✦ To delete characters to the left of the insertion point, press the Backspace key once for each character you want to delete.

✦ To delete characters to the right of the insertion point, press the Delete key once for each character you want to delete.

✦ To delete a block of text, select the text and press the Delete key.

Click the Undo Last Command or Action SmartIcon to cancel a deletion and restore the original text.

Editing Text

Use any of following methods to edit text that you've already entered in a document:

✦ To insert text within existing text (such as missing characters), click where you want the new text to appear and begin typing.

✦ To delete characters to the right of the insertion point, press the Delete key; to delete characters to the left of the insertion point, press the Backspace key.

✦ To type over a group of characters and replace them with new text, select the characters that you want to replace and then type the new characters.

See also the sections "Copying and Moving Text," "Entering Text," and "Selecting Text" in this part.

Entering Text

When you begin typing text in a document, the text appears at the location of the *insertion point* — the blinking cursor that you see in the document area on-screen. Don't confuse the insertion point with the mouse pointer. The mouse pointer normally appears as an I-beam shape in a Word Pro document; use this pointer to click the location in the document where you want to enter text. Follow these steps to enter text in a Word Pro document:

1. Position the insertion point where you want the text to appear. If you've just created a new, blank document, the insertion point is already at the beginning of the first page.

2. Type your text. Keep in mind that you don't need to press Enter at the end of a line. Word Pro automatically wraps your text to the next line when it reaches the end of the current line, and it begins a new page when your text reaches the end of the current page.

To enter text in a SmartMaster template (see "Creating a template-based document," earlier in this part), just click one of the "Click here..." blocks and type the requested information.

You also can use the new ViaVoice feature in Word Pro to automatically enter text in your document by speaking into a microphone. If you want to use this feature (and have the required equipment), but you don't see the ViaVoice menu bar on-screen, you may need to install the feature.

See also "ViaVoice Integration for Word Pro," later in this part.

Finding and Replacing Text

Occasionally you may need to search for specific text in your document or replace existing text with other text. Follow these steps to find and replace text in a document:

1. Place the insertion point where you want to begin your search.

2. Choose Edit⇨Find & Replace Text. The Find & Replace bar appears above the document.

3. In the Find box, type the text you want to search for. If you want to replace that text with other text, type the replacement text in the Replace With box.

4. Select an option from the Find & Replace drop-down list (at the left end of the Find & Replace bar) if you want to narrow your search.

5. Click the right arrow button to search forward in the document or the left arrow button to search backward.

6. If you want to select additional options, click the Options button in the Find & Replace bar. The Find & Replace Text Options dialog box appears. Make the desired selections in this dialog box and then click OK.

7. Click any of the following buttons in the Find & Replace bar:

- Click Find to search for the specified text.

- Click Replace to replace the first occurrence. (The Replace button becomes available only after you click Find and Word Pro finds the text you're searching for.)

- Click Replace All to replace all occurrences.

8. When you're finished, click the Done button to remove the Find & Replace bar.

Formatting

You can improve the appearance of your Word Pro documents by formatting the text. Formatting includes the following: text alignment; attributes such as bold, italics, and underline; borders; line and paragraph spacing; and text font, size, and color. The following sections explain how to apply this formatting in your documents. To quickly remove all text formatting, select the text and then press Ctrl+N.

Adjusting text alignment

You can align text paragraphs to the left, center, or right side of a document. In addition, you can justify the text to align it at both margins. To align text in your document, follow these steps:

1. Place the insertion point at the desired location or select the paragraphs you want to align.

2. Choose Text⇨Text Properties. The Text Properties InfoBox appears.

3. Click the Alignment tab in the InfoBox and then select the alignment option that you want to apply.

Applying bold, underline, or italics

You can add emphasis to selected text in your document by applying the bold, underline, or italic attributes. The easiest way to apply any of these attributes is through the status bar. Follow these steps:

1. Select the text to which you want to apply bold, underline, or italics.

2. Click any of the following buttons on the status bar: Bold (**B**), Italics (*I*), or Underline (U); or press Ctrl+B, Ctrl+I, or Ctrl+U, respectively.

The Bold, Italics, and Underline buttons all act as toggles. To remove these attributes from selected text, click the button in the status bar again. You also can access these and additional text attributes (such as double underline, strikethrough, superscript, and subscript) via the Font, Attribute, and Color tab of the Text Properties InfoBox.

You can apply attributes as you type text. When you're ready to type bold text, for example, click the Bold button in the status bar and then type the text. Click the Bold button again when you're ready to turn off the attribute formatting.

Applying borders

Use the following steps to add a border around a text paragraph:

1. Place the insertion point within the paragraph to which you want to add a border.

2. Choose Text⇨Text Properties. The Text Properties InfoBox appears.

3. Click the Color and Line Style tab in the InfoBox.

4. Click the Lines Around Paragraph button that represents which line borders you want to add; or click the last button in the group of buttons if you want to add a drop shadow to the paragraph.

5. Select the options you want to apply from the drop-down lists in the InfoBox.

6. To see additional options, click the Options button. The Lines & Shadow Options dialog box appears. Select the options that you want and then click OK.

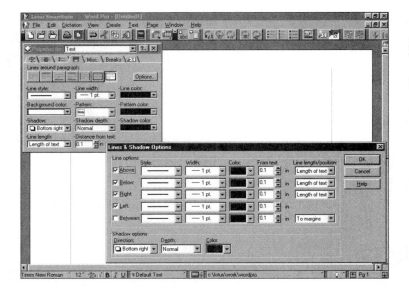

Changing the line spacing

To change the line spacing in a paragraph, follow these steps:

1. Place the insertion point at the desired location or select the paragraphs.

2. Choose Text⇨Text Properties. The Text Properties InfoBox appears.

3. Click the Alignment tab in the InfoBox and then select the option that you want from the Line Spacing drop-down list.

Changing the paragraph spacing

To change the paragraph spacing in a document, follow these steps:

1. Place the insertion point at the desired location or select the paragraphs.

2. Choose Text⇨Text Properties. The Text Properties InfoBox appears.

3. Click the Alignment tab in the InfoBox and then select the options that you want from the Above and Below drop-down lists under Paragraph Spacing.

Changing the text font, size, and color

Use the following steps to apply a different font, size, or color to text in your document:

1. Select the text or paragraphs to which you want to apply a different text font, size, or color.

2. Choose Text⇨Text Properties. The Text Properties InfoBox appears.

3. Click the Font, Attribute, and Color tab in the InfoBox.

4. Select the options that you want from the Font Name and Size lists.

5. To apply a different color to selected text, select the color that you want from the Text Color drop-down list. If you want to use a different background color for the text, select a color from the Background drop-down list.

You can use the three buttons at the left end of the status bar to quickly change the font, size, or color of selected text. Select the text that you want to format and then click the Font button, Size button, or Color button on the status bar. Select the option that you want from the pop-up list that appears.

Headers and Footers

Document headers appear in the top margin of a page, and footers appear in the bottom margin of a page. Headers and footers typically include text such as the document title, page number, and author. Follow these steps to add a header or footer to your document:

1. Click inside the header area (at the top of a page), or the footer area (at the bottom of a page). The Header/Footer bar appears above the document.

2. Click the Cursor Position button that represents the location where you want to enter text.

3. Click the Layout Type button that represents the pages whose margins you want to change. The button on the left is for standard, single-sided documents; the button on the right is for double-sided documents that use facing pages.

4. If you want Word Pro to insert information (such as page numbers) automatically on every page, click the Insert Field button and select a field from the list (such as Date Created, Filename, or Page Number). If you don't want to use any of these preset fields, you can just type the text that you want to appear in the header or footer.

5. To see additional options, click the Header Properties (or Footer Properties) button. In the InfoBox that appears, select the options that you want to apply to the header or footer.

6. When you're finished, click the Done button to remove the Header/Footer bar.

Keyboard Shortcuts

Dozens of keyboard shortcuts are available in Word Pro. The following procedure shows you how to access lists of the shortcut keys within Word Pro's Help system:

1. Choose Help⇨Help Topics. The Help Topics dialog box appears.

2. Click the Contents tab and double-click the topic named Tools For Getting Your Work Done.

3. Double-click the Keyboard And Mouse Shortcuts topic.

4. In the resulting list, double-click the topic relating to the category of keyboard shortcuts that you want to see (such as Keyboard Shortcuts For Commands).

5. View or print the information in the Help window and then click the Close button to close the Help window when you're finished.

See also "Navigating with the keyboard," later in this part.

Moving Around in a Document

When you type or edit text in a document, you must first move the insertion point to the appropriate location in the document. You can use either the keyboard or the mouse to navigate in a document.

Navigating with the keyboard

The following table lists the most common keystrokes for moving around in a document:

Key	Action
← or →	Moves left or right one character
↑ or ↓	Moves up or down one line
PgDn	Moves down one screen
PgUp	Moves up one screen
Ctrl+→	Moves right one word
Ctrl+←	Moves left one word
Home	Moves to the beginning of the current line
End	Moves to the end of the current line
Ctrl+↓	Moves to the beginning of the next paragraph
Ctrl+↑	Moves to the beginning of the current paragraph or to the beginning of the previous paragraph if the cursor is already located at the beginning of a paragraph
Ctrl+ . (period)	Moves to the beginning of the next sentence
Ctrl+ , (comma)	Moves to the beginning of the previous sentence
Ctrl+PgUp	Moves up one document page
Ctrl+PgDn	Moves down one document page
Ctrl+Tab	Moves to the next document
Ctrl+Home	Moves to the beginning of the document (or the current division)
Ctrl+End	Moves to the end of the document (or the current division)

See also "Selecting text with the keyboard," later in this part.

Navigating with the mouse

The following table lists the most common mouse movements for navigating in a document:

Action	Mouse Movement
Move directly to a paragraph	Click the paragraph
Move to a paragraph that's not visible	Use the scroll bars to scroll through the document; click the paragraph when it becomes visible
Move to the previous page or next page in a document	Click the page up or page down arrow at the right end of the status bar

(continued)

(continued)

Action	Mouse Movement
Move to a specific page in the document	Drag the scroll box on the vertical scroll bar until the page gauge displays the page number that you want, or click the Page Status button at the right end of the status bar and select the page number in the Go To dialog box

See also "Selecting text with the mouse," later in this part.

Numbered Lists

Use numbered lists to present sequential information in your documents. To enter a numbered list in your document, use the following steps:

1. Position the insertion point where you want to begin a numbered list.

2. Click the Insert Default Number SmartIcon. The first number appears in the document.

3. Type the text for the first numbered item and then press Enter to begin the next numbered item.

4. After typing the final numbered item, press Enter and then click the Insert Default Number SmartIcon again to turn off the numbered list formatting.

To insert new numbered paragraphs in the middle of a numbered list, position the insertion point at the end of a numbered paragraph and press Enter. The number formatting carries to the new paragraph, and all following paragraphs are automatically renumbered.

To skip numbering a paragraph within a numbered list, click the Skip Bullet/Number SmartIcon, type the text of the paragraph, and then press Enter. Click this SmartIcon again to resume the numbered list.

To change the appearance or other properties of a numbered list, follow these steps:

1. Select the numbered list and then choose Text⇨Text Properties to display the Text Properties InfoBox.

2. Click the Bullet And Number tab in the InfoBox.

3. In the InfoBox, click the button representing the number style you want to use and then select any other options you want to apply. Click the Custom button in the InfoBox to access additional number formatting options.

To add numbers to (or remove numbers from) existing paragraphs of text, select the paragraphs and then click the Insert Default Number SmartIcon.

See also "Bulleted Lists," earlier in this part.

Printing

When you're ready to print your document, you should first preview what you want to print. You can print an entire document, specified pages or divisions, or any text or object that you select. You can use the default print settings to quickly print one copy of a document, or you can use the InfoBox and Print dialog box to customize the print and page settings.

See also "InfoBoxes" in Part II.

Changing the page layout

You can change page layout options, such as the margins and orientation of your document before you print. Follow these steps:

1. Choose Page⇨Page Properties. The Page Properties InfoBox appears.

2. Click the Size and Margin tab in the InfoBox.

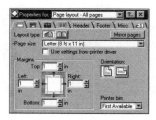

3. Click the Layout Type button representing the type of layout you want to use. The button on the left is for standard, single-sided documents; the button on the right is for double-sided documents that use facing pages.

4. Edit the margin settings in the Top, Left, Right, and Bottom boxes.

5. Click the button representing the print orientation that you want to use.

6. Select other options in the Page Properties InfoBox (including options on other tabs), as desired.

To add a fancy border surrounding your document, click the Color, Pattern, and Line Style tab in the Page Properties InfoBox. Then select a border from the Designer Border drop-down list.

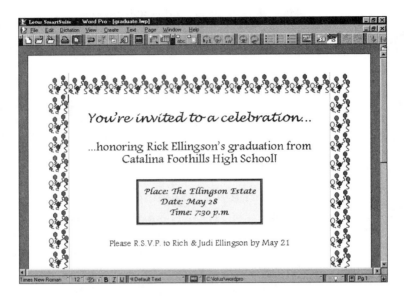

Inserting page breaks

Word Pro inserts page breaks for you automatically when you type more than one page of text. However, you sometimes may want to insert manual page breaks at a location that you specify. Follow these steps:

1. Place the insertion point where you want a new page to begin.

2. Choose Page⇨Insert Page Break (or press Ctrl+Enter). A page break is inserted in the document. The page break appears as a gray horizontal line with a page icon at the left end of the line.

To remove a manual page break, position the insertion point at the left end of the page break line and choose Page⇨Delete Page Break. To access additional page break options, choose Text⇨ Text Properties and click the Breaks tab.

Previewing a document

To preview the current page of a document on-screen and see how it will look when printed, just click the Zoom to Full Page SmartIcon. Click this SmartIcon again to return to the previous view. If you want to preview two facing pages on-screen at once, choose View⇨Facing Pages.

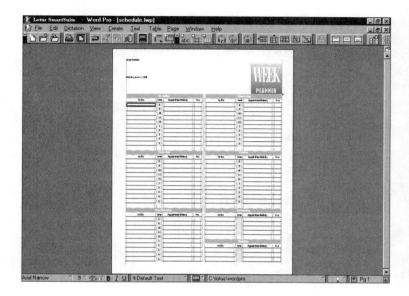

Printing a document

Follow these steps when you're ready to print your document:

1. Open (or switch to) the document that you want to print.

2. Choose File⇨Print or click the Print SmartIcon. The Print dialog box appears.

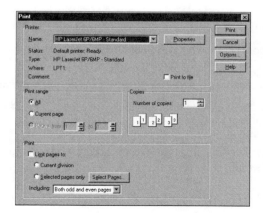

3. In the Printer area, select the printer that you want to use. Your default printer should already be selected. If you want to print your document to a file rather than to the printer, select the Print To Fi_le check box.

4. In the Print Range area, select the pages that you want to print (or keep the default of _All Pages).

5. If you don't want to print the entire document, select what you want to print in the Print area.

6. In the Copies area, select the Number Of _Copies you want to print. If you're printing multiple pages, you can also select the C_ollate option.

7. Click the Opt_ions button. The Print Options dialog box appears.

8. Select the Print Options and Update Options that you want to use (if any) and then click OK.

9. Click the Print button (or press Enter) to begin printing.

If you just want to print a quick copy of the current document to the default printer, click the Print SmartIcon and then click the Print button in the Print dialog box.

Printing envelopes

The Envelope bar makes it simple for you to create and print envelopes in Word Pro. Follow these steps:

1. Open an existing envelope document or a blank document.

2. Choose _Create⇨Enve_lope. The Envelope bar appears above the document, and Word Pro inserts a new page in the document.

3. Click in the designated address locations of the envelope document and then type the addresses; or click the _Send To Address and _Return Address buttons on the Envelope bar and select the addresses from a list (if you've added addresses to this list).

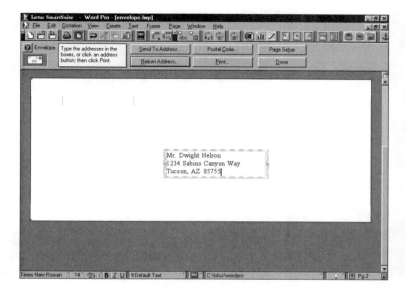

4. If you need to adjust the page setup, click the Page Setup button in the Envelope bar and make your selections.

5. Click the Print button in the Envelope bar. The Print dialog box appears.

6. Make any additional selections and then click the Print button to print the envelope.

7. When you're finished, click the Done button to remove the Envelope bar.

Printing labels

You can use a Word Pro SmartMaster to print labels. Follow these steps:

1. Choose File⇨New Document or click the Create a New Document SmartIcon. The New Document dialog box appears.

2. Click the Create From Any SmartMaster tab.

3. In the Select A Type Of SmartMaster list box, select Label.

4. In the Select A Look list box, select the file named LABEL.MWP and then click OK. The Create Labels dialog box appears.

5. In the list box, select the Avery label number that you want to use. If you're using a different brand of labels, select a label number that has the same dimensions as the Avery labels.

The dimensions appear in the lower-right corner of the dialog box when you select a label type.

6. Click the Create button. The label form appears on-screen.

7. Type the text that you want to appear on the first label and then press Tab to move to the next label. When you press Tab at the end of a row, Word Pro inserts a new row of labels and places the cursor in the first label of the new row.

8. When you're ready to print the labels, click the Print SmartIcon and then click the Print button in the dialog box.

See also "Copying text," earlier in this part.

Proofing Documents

After you create and format your document, you may want to use one or more tools in Word Pro to proof your document. You can run a spell check, run a grammar check, and look up synonyms using the Thesaurus.

Checking the Thesaurus

Can't think of that perfect word you want to use in your document? Try using the Thesaurus in Word Pro to look up synonyms. Follow these steps:

1. Position the insertion point in the word you want to look up.

2. Choose Edit➪Proofing Tools➪Check Thesaurus. The Thesaurus dialog box appears.

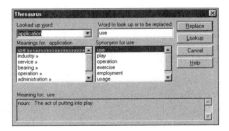

3. If you see a word in the Synonyms list that you want to use, select that word and then click the Replace button. If you don't want to use a word from the Synonyms list, select another word in the Meanings For list to display additional synonyms. You also can select a synonym and click the Lookup button to display even more choices. When you see the word you want, select it and click Replace.

4. Click the Cancel button to close the dialog box and return to the Word Pro document.

Running a grammar check

To run a grammar check in a document, follow these steps:

1. Position the insertion point where you want to begin the grammar check.

2. Choose Edit⇨Proofing Tools⇨Check Grammar. The Grammar Check bar appears above the document.

3. If Word Pro finds possible grammatical errors in your document, the first error appears in the Grammar Check bar. If you don't understand the error, click the Explain button for more information.

4. At this point, you can click Replace or Skip or click inside the document if you want to edit the item yourself. Repeat this step for each error that Word Pro displays.

5. Click the Done button to remove the Grammar Check bar, and then click the Close button to close the Readability Statistics dialog box.

Spell checking your document

To run a spell check in an existing document, follow these steps:

1. Position the insertion point where you want to begin the spell check.

2. Choose Edit⇨Check Spelling or click the Check Spelling SmartIcon. The Spell Check bar appears above the document, and Word Pro highlights the possible misspellings in the document.

3. If you see another word in the Spell Check bar that you want to use in place of the highlighted word, select that word and click Replace or Replace All, as appropriate. If the highlighted word is spelled correctly, click Skip to skip this occurrence or click Skip All to skip all occurrences of this word in the document. (You also can click the word in the document and type the correction.)

4. Repeat Step 3 for each highlighted word.

5. Click the Done button to remove the Spell Check bar.

If you prefer to correct spelling errors as you type in a document, you can use the Spell Check button on the status bar. A question mark appears on the Spell Check button if Word Pro doesn't recognize a word that you type. When this happens, click the Spell Check button and select the correct spelling (or choose another option).

Selecting Text

In most cases, you need to select text before you do anything that affects the text (such as formatting, editing, copying, moving, or deleting). You can use either the keyboard or the mouse to select text in Word Pro.

Always be careful when selecting a large amount of text — anything you type will automatically replace the selection! If this happens and you catch it right away, you can click the Undo SmartIcon to reverse the action.

Selecting text with the keyboard

To select text with the keyboard, use the navigation keys (such as the arrow keys, PgUp, or PgDn) to move to the location where you want to begin selecting text. Then press and hold down the Shift key and use the navigation keys to extend the selection to the word, sentence, paragraph, or entire document.

See also "Navigating with the keyboard," earlier in this part.

Selecting text with the mouse

To use the mouse to select text, click in the document where you want to begin selecting text. Then drag to the end of the text that you want to select and release the mouse button.

You also can use the following mouse tricks to quickly select words, sentences, or paragraphs in a document:

To Select This:	Do This:
A word	Double-click the word.
A sentence	Hold down the Ctrl key and click in the sentence.
A paragraph	Hold down the Ctrl key and double-click in the paragraph.
Any amount of text	Click at the beginning of the text and then hold down the Shift key and click the end of the text.

See also "Navigating with the mouse," earlier in this part.

Styles

A *style* is a collection of formatting attributes that can be applied as a group to a paragraph. You can apply styles using the status bar, InfoBox, or keyboard shortcuts. Word Pro includes many built-in styles, but you also have the option of creating your own styles.

Applying styles to paragraphs

To apply a style to a paragraph, follow these steps:

1. Position the insertion point in the paragraph to which you want to apply a style.

2. Click the Style button in the status bar.

3. Select the style that you want from the Style pop-up list. The style you select is applied to the paragraph.

Creating new styles

To create a new style, you must first format a paragraph using all the attributes that you want to include in your style. After you do this, follow these steps to create a new style:

1. Select the paragraph that you want to use to create the new style.

2. Choose Text⇨Text Properties. The Text Properties InfoBox appears.

3. Click the Style tab in the InfoBox and then click the Create Style button.

4. Type a Style Name and Description in the text boxes.

5. In the Style Type drop-down list, select the type of style that you want to create (such as Paragraph or Character).

6. Click OK. The new style now appears in the Style list in the InfoBox. You can also access this new style from the Style button in the status bar.

Tables

Tables display Word Pro information in a grid that contains rows and columns — similar to a spreadsheet. When you create a table, you specify how many rows and columns you want to use (most tables include just a few of each). You can add a table and then type the text that goes in the table, or you can create a table based on existing text.

Creating a table

To create a table in your document, follow these steps:

1. Position the insertion point where you want the table to appear in the document.

 2. Click the Create Table Grid SmartIcon. A table grid drops down from the SmartIcon bar.

3. Drag inside the grid to select the number of columns and rows that you want to include in the table.

4. Release the mouse button. The table appears in the document, and the insertion point is positioned in the first table cell.

To create a table based on existing text, follow these steps:

1. Select the text that you want to place in the table. The text you select should use tabs to separate columnar data and hard returns (separate paragraphs) to separate rows.

2. Choose Create⇨Table.

3. Click Yes to confirm that you want to convert the selected text to a table.

Inserting text in a table

Follow these steps to insert text in your table:

1. Click the table cell in which you want to enter text.

2. Type the text and then press the Tab key to move to the next cell. You also can use the arrow keys to move between cells.

3. When you've typed text in the last cell of the table, press Tab to insert a new row, or click outside the table if you're finished.

 When you click inside a table, you see a Table option added to Word Pro's main menu. Use the options available on this menu to format tables and modify their structure.

Tabs and Indents

You use tabs and indents in Word Pro to help place and align text in your documents. Word Pro provides several options for indenting text paragraphs. You choose the indent options from the Text Properties InfoBox. Tabs can align text on the left, right, or center of a tab mark. You also can use the numeric tab to align decimals in a column of numbers. By default, Word Pro includes tab stops at every one-half inch in a document. You can use these tabs or insert your own tabs at any location. Tabs are displayed as red tick marks on the ruler.

Indenting paragraphs

Follow these steps to change the indentation in a paragraph:

1. Position the insertion point in the paragraph.

2. Choose Text⇨Text Properties to display the Text Properties InfoBox.

3. Click the Alignment tab in the InfoBox. The Indent options appear on the left side of the Alignment tab (just below the Alignment buttons).

4. Click the Indent button representing the type of indent that you want to apply to the paragraph. These four buttons indent all lines of text from the left margin, just the first line, all lines except the first line, and all lines From both margins.

5. If you want to change the amount of indentation from the margins, type the new number in the Indent From Margin box.

6. For additional indent options, click the Options button, select the desired options, and then click OK.

If you want to remove the indentation from a paragraph, click the No Indent button on the Alignment tab of the Text Properties InfoBox.

See also "Adjusting text alignment," earlier in this part.

Setting tabs

To insert new tab stops in a paragraph, follow these steps:

1. Position the insertion point in the paragraph.

2. If the ruler doesn't already appear above the document, click the Show/Hide Ruler SmartIcon to display it.

3. Right-click inside the ruler and choose the option for the type of tab that you want to insert: Left, Right, Centered, or Numeric.

4. Click inside the ruler where you want the new tab stop to appear. A tab marker arrow appears inside the ruler.

To move a tab stop, drag it to another location in the ruler. To delete a tab stop, drag it off of the ruler. To remove all tab stops that you've added to a paragraph, right-click the ruler and choose Clear All Tabs.

ViaVoice for Word Pro

ViaVoice is an exciting new speech recognition feature in Word Pro Millennium Edition that enables you to record dictation and convert your spoken words into typed text! After you dictate your document, you can then edit the document as necessary to fix any misspellings or misinterpretations. You can play back your voice recording or have the computer read the text back to you.

ViaVoice has more strict hardware requirements than the other applications in SmartSuite. The following are the minimum hardware requirements for ViaVoice:

+ Pentium 150 MHz processor with MMX (or a Pentium 166 MHz without MMX)

+ CD-ROM drive

+ VGA adapter and monitor

+ Sound card

+ Microphone (included with the SmartSuite package)

+ 125MB of available disk space and 32MB of RAM (or 48MB of RAM in Windows NT)

Installing ViaVoice

If your computer meets the above requirements but you don't see the ViaVoice SpeechBar (or the Dictation option in the menu bar) when you start Word Pro, you need to install ViaVoice. Follow these steps:

1. Insert the SmartSuite CD in your CD-ROM drive.

2. Click the Start button in the Windows taskbar; then choose Programs➪Windows Explorer.

3. Select the CD-ROM drive letter and then double-click the Extra folder.

4. Click the Viavoice folder and then double-click the SETUP.EXE file.

5. Follow the prompts to set up the ViaVoice feature on your system.

Using ViaVoice

To begin using ViaVoice to dictate a document, follow these steps:

1. If the ViaVoice SpeechBar doesn't appear at the top of your screen, choose <u>D</u>ictation⇨<u>S</u>tart ViaVoice.

2. To view a list of voice commands, speak "What can I say?" clearly into your microphone. The command list appears on-screen. Press Esc to remove the command list.

If the command list doesn't appear, make sure that your microphone is turned on. The Microphone button must be green (on) or yellow (sleeping). If the button is gray, click it to turn on the microphone.

⌐ViaVoice SpeechBar

Microphone button

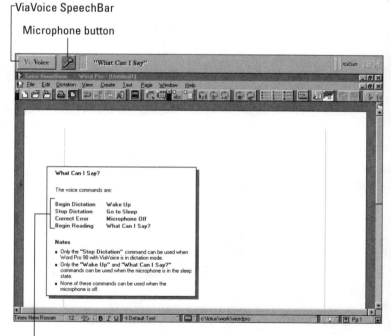

List of voice commands

3. When you're ready to dictate your document, speak the words "Begin dictation" into the microphone.

4. Dictate the words that you want to appear in your document. Be sure to speak clearly!

5. When you're finished dictating your document, speak the words "Stop dictation" into the microphone.

If you find errors or misinterpretations in the text that appears in the document, select the text (no more than ten words) and then choose Dictation⇨Correct Error. Type the correct text and click OK (or choose another option from the pop-up menu).

To hear your voice played back through your computer's speakers, select the text that you want to play back and then choose Dictation⇨Playback. To hear the computer read your document back to you, select the text and then speak "Begin reading" (or choose Dictation⇨Begin Reading). A character (referred to as an *actor*) appears on-screen as it reads the text.

You can use the Reading options to change the actor and even the sound of the voice used to read text! Follow these steps:

1. Choose Dictation⇨Reading Options. The Virtual Voices Control Properties dialog box appears.

2. Click the Voice Models tab to select the speaking voice that you want to use. The default voice is an English-American adult male.

3. To change the actor used to read text, click the Actor Gallery tab and then select the actor from the scrolling list. The default actor is Woodrow, the pencil. In the following dialog box, Kingsley, the robot, is selected.

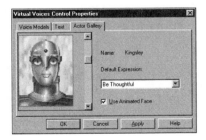

4. Click OK to close the dialog box.

You can find additional ViaVoice features by clicking the ViaVoice button in the SpeechBar or by choosing the Dictation option in the menu bar. To access Help information on ViaVoice, choose Help⇨ViaVoice Help Topics. For additional technical support on ViaVoice for Word Pro, visit the Lotus Web site at www.lotus.com.

Viewing Documents

You can display your document using a variety of on-screen views —Draft view, Layout view, Outline view, and Page Sorter view. In Word Pro, you access these views and other special views from the View menu.

To find more view options that affect what you see on-screen (such as margin guides, ruler, and divider tabs), choose View⇨ Set View Preferences and click the Show (or Clean Screen) tab. For additional view options, choose File⇨User Setup⇨Word Pro Preferences and click the Enable tab in the Word Pro Preferences dialog box.

See also "Window Displays" in Part II.

Draft view

In Draft view, the document window fills the screen, and text wraps to the size of the window. You still see text formatting and page breaks, but you don't see any graphics, headers, or footers. Don't worry — they're still there! Just switch to Layout view to see them again.

To display your document in Draft view, choose View⇨Draft.

Layout view

Layout view displays all graphics, text formatting, page breaks, headers, and footers in your document. You'll probably use this view most often because it displays a document on-screen almost exactly as it will appear when printed.

To display your document in Layout view, choose View⇨Layout.

Outline view

The display that you see in Outline view is similar to Draft view — you primarily see text, with no graphics or page breaks. While in Outline view, you can more easily rearrange text and change heading levels.

To display your document in Outline view, follow these steps:

1. Choose View⇨Outline. The Outline bar appears above the document.

2. Use the tools in the Outline bar to edit or manipulate your outline. For more information on these tools, click the question mark button at the left end of the Outline bar.

3. When you're finished using Outline view, click the <u>D</u>one button in the Outline bar. Word Pro switches back to the previous view.

Page Sorter view

Page Sorter view provides an overall view of the pages in your presentation. You see smaller versions of several pages on-screen at one time, along with the page numbers. Use the scroll bars to view additional pages, if necessary. This view is also useful if you need to rearrange pages in your document.

To display your document in Page Sorter view, choose <u>V</u>iew⇨<u>P</u>age Sorter. If you see a plus sign in the upper-left corner of a page, click the plus sign to see additional pages or divisions in Page Sorter view. Click the minus sign to collapse pages or divisions.

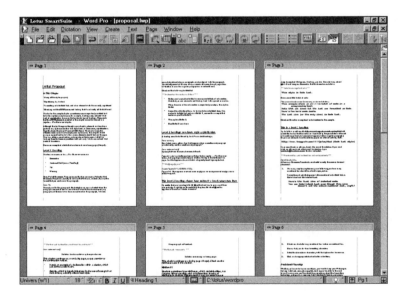

Special views

Word Pro also provides several special views that combine two or more of the views described in the previous sections. To use one of the special views, choose <u>V</u>iew⇨<u>S</u>pecial Views. Select the view that you want to use from the dialog box and then click OK.

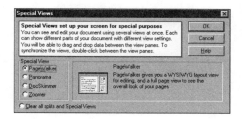

Zooming Documents

You can specify a percentage by which to enlarge or shrink the document display. Change the magnification to a larger percentage to enlarge the text. To shrink the text and display more text on-screen at one time, use a smaller zoom percentage. Changing the zoom percentage has no effect on printing. Choose from these options:

✦ Choose View⇨Zoom To. Select a percentage to switch to a specified zoom level, or use the Page Width or Margin Width options to fill the document window (with or without margins displayed, respectively).

✦ Choose View⇨Zoom To Custom Level to switch the zoom back to the custom level (91% by default).

To change the custom zoom level, choose View⇨Zoom To⇨Other. Then change the Custom Level % to the desired percentage and click OK.

Part V

Freelance Graphics

Freelance Graphics, the presentation graphics package included with Lotus SmartSuite Millennium Edition, helps you create stunning presentations with very little effort — especially if you use SmartMasters and content topics to create your presentation. SmartMaster templates get you started with the look of your presentation; content topics further automate the process by providing actual content for typical presentation topics, such as business plans and project proposals. You can display your presentation as a screen show, on overhead transparencies or 35mm slides, on printed pages, or via the Internet.

In this part . . .

- ✔ **Spicing up your presentations with charts and clip art**
- ✔ **Creating and running a presentation**
- ✔ **Understanding the output options available**
- ✔ **Adding sound and visual effects to your presentation**
- ✔ **Switching among the different Freelance views**

Charts

If you need to present numerical data, you may want to add a chart to a page of your Freelance Graphics presentation. Charts can get your point across much more quickly than a table of numbers. After you create a chart, you can easily edit or format the chart to improve its appearance.

Adding charts to a presentation

You use the Create Chart dialog box to select the chart type, chart style, and chart colors. Follow these steps to add a chart to your presentation:

1. Use one of the following methods to display the Create Chart dialog box:

   • Choose <u>C</u>reate⇨Cha<u>r</u>t.

    • Click the Create a Chart SmartIcon.

   • Click the New Page button to create a new page and select a page layout that includes a chart (such as Bullets & Chart); then click the Click Here To Create Chart block.

2. When the Create Chart dialog box appears, select a chart type (such as Bar) in the first list box and then click one of the icons beside this list box. These icons control the orientation and 3D options for the selected chart type.

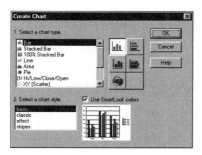

3. In the second list box, select a chart style. A preview of the chart appears to the right of the list box.

4. Click OK. The Edit Data dialog box appears. You have two options for entering your chart data:

   • Type the data for your chart directly in the Edit Data dialog box.

- Click the Import Data button if you want to import the chart data from a worksheet or file. If you choose this option, select the file that you want and click Open to return to the Edit Data dialog box. Make any necessary corrections to the imported data.

5. A preview of the chart appears at the top of the Edit Data dialog box. Click OK to close the dialog box and view the chart on the page.

Editing and formatting charts

After you create a chart, you can change the chart type, edit the chart, or add information to the chart (such as a chart title). You also can format the chart by changing colors and patterns and modifying the text fonts.

To switch to another chart type, follow these steps:

1. Display the page containing the chart and choose Chart⇨Chart Type. The Chart Properties InfoBox appears.

2. In the Type tab of the Chart Properties InfoBox, select the new chart type. (If you want to also change the chart style, use the Named Styles tab.) Your changes are immediately reflected on the page.

To edit or format the chart, follow these steps:

1. Display the page containing the chart.

2. Use any of the following options to edit the chart:

- Double-click the chart to display the Chart Properties InfoBox. In the Properties For drop-down list, select the option representing the portion of the chart that you want to change (such as Legend). Then select the options that you want (or type text, if applicable).

- Right-click the portion of the chart that you want to edit. Then make your selection from the context-sensitive shortcut menu that appears.

- Click the chart once to select it. Then open the Chart menu and choose the appropriate option from the drop-down menu.

See also "InfoBoxes" in Part II.

Clip Art and Drawn Objects

You can add clip art or drawn objects such as a company logo, cartoon, or business graphic to your presentation pages. Clip art usually consists of multiple pre-drawn graphic objects that are grouped together and treated as a single object. Clip art can also be imported bitmaps or charts. Drawn objects include rectangles, ellipses, and freehand drawings. Freelance Graphics provides shapes that allow you to add text inside them.

Adding clip art to a presentation

Follow these steps to add clip art to a single page of your presentation:

1. In the Current Page view, click the Clip Art button; or click a Click Here To Add Clip Art block on a page. The Add Clip Art Or Diagram To The Page dialog box appears.

2. Select a clip art category from the Category drop-down list. You also can click the button with four triangles (at the bottom of the dialog box) to scan through the categories. If you choose this option, click the stop button (the square) when you see the category you want.

3. Use the forward and back triangle buttons to view additional clip art images in the selected category; then click the clip art you want to use.

4. Click OK to insert the clip art image.

See also "Current Page view," later in this part.

You also can add clip art or any other object to all the pages in your presentation. Follow these steps:

1. Choose Presentation⇨Add a Logo to Every Page. You see a page in Current Layout view.

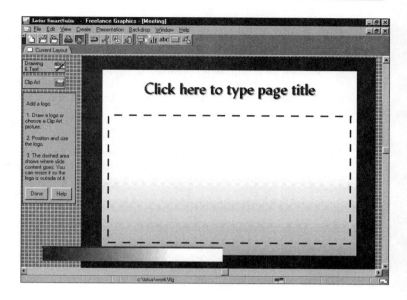

2. Follow the instructions provided on the left side of the screen to add a logo or clip art image to a blank area of the page. If you want to insert an image from the clip art library, choose Create⇔Add Clip Art or click the Clip Art button.

3. Click Done when you're finished.

Your logo or clip art image may overlap existing text or graphics if you don't place the image in a blank area of the page. If necessary, you can resize the dashed area (in the Current Layout view) to make it smaller so that you can place the image outside this area of the page.

Adding drawn objects

If you want to add a drawn object to a page of your presentation, you can use the drawing tools. Click the Drawing & Text button in Current Page view to access these tools. The drawing tools include Tools, Shapes with text, and Connectors. Most often, you'll probably use the Tools buttons to create objects such as arrows, lines, circles, ellipses, squares, rectangles, and freehand objects.

The following steps show you how to use the drawing tools to draw a rectangle or a square. Follow similar procedures to create other types of objects.

1. In Current Page view, click the Drawing & Text button. The Drawing Tools palette appears on-screen.

2. Click the Rectangle button in the Tools section of the palette. (If you plan to add text inside the rectangle, click the Rectangle button in the Shapes With Text area of the palette.)

3. To draw a rectangle, position the pointer at the starting point of the rectangle and, holding down the mouse button, drag the pointer to the opposite corner. Release the mouse button.

To resize a drawn object, click the object to select it and then drag the sizing handles. To add text inside an object (if you chose an object in the Shapes With Text area of the Drawing Tools palette), double-click the object and type the text; then click OK. The object resizes to fit the text you type. To change other attributes of an object (such as color), double-click the object and make the selections from the InfoBox.

See also "Current Page view," later in this part.

Creating a Presentation

Creating a new presentation in Freelance Graphics is straightforward, especially if you use one of the SmartMaster templates to get started. SmartMasters include content topics, presentation looks, and page layouts. Content topics provide actual text for common types of business presentations. A presentation look is a collection of page layouts, all displaying the same background design. In addition to using a SmartMaster, you also have the option of creating a blank presentation, with no background design or content suggestions.

For steps to help you begin a new presentation, go to the "Starting a new presentation" section in this part.

If you need help while working on your presentation, click the Guide Me button (near the top-right corner of the screen) at any time. Click one of the tasks listed, or click the Help Topics button to display the Help Topics dialog box.

See also "Help Information" in Part II.

Adding and editing page content

When you create a presentation, some of the pages may include "Click here..." text blocks that you can use to enter the text that you want. To enter text in a "Click here..." text box, just click the box, type your text, and click OK. Adding text is as simple as that! When you're done typing text, press Escape or click anywhere outside the text block.

If you want to see tips while you're entering (or editing) text, click the Tips button; then click OK to close the Tips box.

You can use the drawing tools to insert additional text blocks in any page of your presentation. To add a new text block, follow these steps:

1. In Current Page view, display the page that you want to edit.

2. Click the Drawing & Text button. The drawing tools appear.

3. Click the Text button (the "abc" button) in the Drawing Tools box; then click and drag to create a text box in a blank area of the page where you want the text block to appear.

4. Enter the new text.

5. Click OK when you're finished entering the text.

If your presentation includes content pages with text already filled in for you, you can accept the existing content or change it to suit your own needs. You also can edit text that you've previously entered in a text block. To edit page content, follow these steps:

1. In Current Page view, display the page that you want to edit.

2. Double-click the text block at the location where you want to edit the text.

3. Edit the text.

4. Click OK when you're finished editing the text.

If you've added a new page and want to switch to a different page layout, display the page and then click the Page Layout button in the status bar. Select the layout that you want to switch to and then click OK.

See also "Current Page view," later in this part, and "Editing Text," in Part IV.

Changing the page order

Need to organize the pages of your presentation? The easiest way to do so is to rearrange the pages while in Page Sorter view. Follow these steps to change the page order:

1. Click the Page Sorter tab.

2. Click the page that you want to move. If you want to select multiple pages, hold down the Shift key and click each additional page.

3. Drag the page to a new position. A vertical bar shows you where the page will be inserted; release the mouse button at the desired location.

If you want to create a copy of an existing page, hold down the Ctrl key as you drag the page to another position. A new page is added to the presentation; edit the new page as necessary.

See also "Page Sorter view," later in this part.

Opening an existing presentation file

When you start Freelance Graphics, the Welcome To Lotus Freelance Graphics dialog box appears, and you're given the option to open an existing presentation file. To do so, click the name of the presentation in the list box and click OK. If you don't see the presentation you want, use the Browse button to find it.

If you're already running Freelance Graphics, you can open a presentation by using the Open dialog box.

See also "Opening a File," in Part II.

Running a screen show

Before you present an on-screen presentation to others, you should run through the screen show at least a few times so that you can understand how the procedure works and how your presentation will look to others. Follow these steps to run your screen show:

1. Choose Presentation⇨Run Screen Show⇨From Beginning (or click the Run Screen Show from Beginning SmartIcon).

If you prefer to run the screen show from the current page instead, choose Presentation⇨Run Screen Show⇨ From Current Page.

2. The first (or current) page of the screen show is displayed full-screen. At this point, you can perform any of the actions in the following table:

To Accomplish This	Perform This Action
Advance to the next page	Click the left mouse button, press PgDn, or press Enter
Return to the previous page	Click the right mouse button and choose Previous, press PgUp, or press Backspace
Jump to another page	Press Esc, select the page in the Page To Go To box, and click the Go To Page button
Pause and resume the screen show	Press Spacebar (if pages are set to advance automatically)
Quit the screen show	Press Esc and click the Quit Screen Show button

While you're running a screen show, you can also display a shortcut menu that provides several additional options to help you control the presentation. Follow these steps:

 1. Choose Presentation⇨Run Screen Show⇨From Beginning.

2. Right-click anywhere on-screen to display the shortcut menu.

3. Choose from the following options on the shortcut menu:

Shortcut Menu Option	Action
Next	Moves to the next page
Previous	Returns to the previous page
Go To	Moves to a page that you specify
Allow Drawing	Displays an on-screen drawing
Pen Color	Lets you choose the draw color: Red, Green, Blue, Yellow, Cyan, Magenta, Black, White, or Gray
Pen Width	Lets you choose how wide the pen draws: Thin, Medium, or Thick
Speaker Notes	Allows you to create or edit speaker notes for the current page
Control Panel	Lets you hide or display the control panel or choose the corner of the screen in which it displays
End Screen Show	Stops the screen show

You can set up your show to run automatically, without interaction from you. This feature is useful for running a continuous presentation at a trade show booth. Choose Presentation⇨Set Up Screen Show. On the Page Effects tab, select the After 3 Seconds option and click OK. You can choose a different number of seconds between pages by typing the number you want in the text box.

Starting a new presentation

You can start a new presentation from the Welcome to Lotus Freelance Graphics dialog box that appears when you start the program, or from the New Presentation dialog box. Follow these steps to create a new presentation:

1. If you don't see the Welcome to Lotus Freelance Graphics dialog box on-screen, choose File⇨New Presentation (or click the Create a New Presentation SmartIcon). The New Presentation dialog box appears.

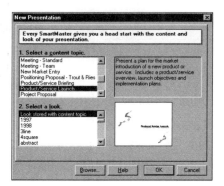

2. In the Select A Content Topic list box, choose the content topic that you want to use in your presentation. A description of the selected topic appears in the gray box beside the list. If none of the items in the list applies to your type of presentation, select [No Content Topic] at the top of the list.

3. In the Select A Look list box, choose the look that you want to use in your presentation. (If you chose a content topic in the preceding step, Freelance suggests a look for that topic; you may prefer to use another look.) A preview of the selected design appears to the right of the list.

4. Click OK. The New Page dialog box appears.

5. If you chose a content topic in Step 2 above, you see a two-tabbed New Page dialog box. On the Content Pages tab, select a specific content topic from the list; if you want to select more than one content topic, click the Choose <u>M</u>ultiple Content Pages button and follow the instructions on-screen.

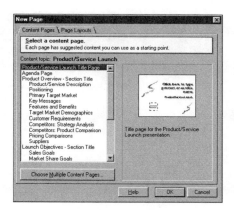

As an alternative to choosing a specific content page, you can click the Page Layouts tab and select a generic page layout with no predefined content.

If you chose [No Content Topic] in Step 2 above, you see the New Page dialog box with available page layouts. Choose the page layout that you want (such as Title, for a title page).

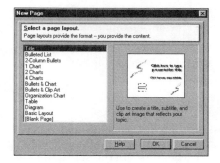

6. Click OK. The page you selected appears on-screen.

7. Click the "Click here..." blocks that appear on the page and enter the requested information.

 Each time that you want to add another page to the presentation, click the New Page button (in Current Page view) and select another content page or page layout; then click OK and enter the appropriate information on the page.

 You can find additional SmartMaster content topics and looks on the SmartSuite CD. Use the Custom Installation option and navigate to the appropriate Freelance Graphics screen that lists these items.

See also "Current Page view," later in this part.

Keyboard Shortcuts

Dozens of keyboard shortcuts are available in Freelance Graphics to help you create and edit your presentations. The following steps show you how to access lists of the shortcut keys within the Freelance Graphics Help system:

   1. Choose Help⇨Help Topics. The Help Topics dialog box appears.

   2. Click the Contents tab and double-click the topic named Tools For Getting Your Work Done.

3. Double-click the Keyboard And Mouse Shortcuts topic.

4. In the resulting list, double-click the topic relating to the category of shortcuts that you want to see (such as Navigating In A Text Block).

5. View or print the information in the Help window; then click the Close button to close the window when you're finished.

Printing

You can print your presentation using the following formats: as one or more presentation pages on each printed page, as one to three presentation pages with accompanying speaker notes or audience notes on each printed page, or as an outline. You also can add a border to the pages. Other methods of outputting your presentation include 35mm slides, printing to a file, and even publishing your presentation to the Web!

See also "Saving a Freelance Graphics presentation as Web pages" In Part IX.

Generating 35mm slides

You can create 35mm slides of your presentation by sending your presentation file to a slide service. Before you do so, you must optimize the screen and printed output for 35mm slides. Follow these steps:

1. Choose File➪Setup for 35mm Slides. The Setup for 35mm Slides dialog box appears.

2. Select the Adjust Page Size And Color Output For 35mm Slides check box and click OK.

Freelance Graphics adjusts the dimensions of the pages and selects an appropriate color scheme for 35mm slides.

After performing this procedure, be sure to carefully check each page in the presentation. You may see unexpected results that need to be corrected before submitting your presentation file to a slide service. You also should check with the slide service to make sure that it can use the slides in the format that you plan to use.

If you've already optimized your presentation for 35mm slides and later want to print it using another form of output, choose File➪Setup for 35mm Slides and uncheck the check box.

Previewing a presentation

Before you print a presentation, you should always preview the
pages in your presentation to see how they'll look when printed.
Follow these steps:

1. Choose File⇨Print Preview (or click the Print Preview
SmartIcon). The Print Preview dialog box appears.

2. Select whether you want to begin the preview with the First
Page or the Current Page; then click OK.

3. Click the Next or Previous button to move between pages
in the presentation. To move to a specific page, press
Esc, choose Go To, and double-click the slide that you want
to view.

4. Click the Quit button to end the preview or the Print button to
display the Print dialog box.

Printing a presentation

When you're ready to print the presentation, you can print the
current page, a range of pages, or your entire presentation. Use
the following steps to print a presentation:

1. Choose File⇨Print (or click the Print SmartIcon). The Print
dialog box appears.

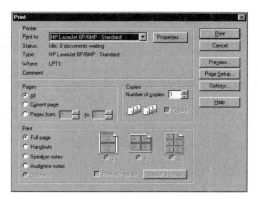

2. In the Pages area, select the pages that you want to print.

3. If you want to print more than one copy of the presentation,
type the number you want in the Number Of Copies text box.

4. In the Print area, specify the format of the printed output.

5. Click the Print button to begin printing.

Before you print to a black and white printer, click the Color/B&W button that appears in the status bar (to the left of the Page Layout button). This button gives you a preview of how your presentation pages will look when printed in black and white.

To add headers and/or footers to your printed pages, choose File⇨Page Setup (or click the Page Setup button in the Print dialog box). Follow the instructions in the Page Setup dialog box and then click OK.

Save and Go Feature

Freelance Graphics provides the Save and Go feature for those of you who need to take your presentations with you on the road. This feature compresses and saves presentations to floppy disks or another format. When you arrive at your destination, you can decompress the presentation files and show your presentation on another computer. If that computer doesn't have Freelance Graphics installed, you can use the Mobile Screen Show Player to run the screen show.

Follow these steps to use Save and Go:

1. Choose File⇨Save and Go. The Save and Go - Introduction dialog box appears.

2. Read the instructions in the dialog box and then click Next to continue.

3. In the Save and Go - Select a Presentation dialog box, specify which presentation you want to save and then click Next.

4. In the Save and Go - Select a Name and Destination dialog box, choose a name and destination for the compressed file and then click Next.

5. In the Save and Go - Include Mobile Screen Show Player dialog box, specify whether you want to include the Mobile Screen Show Player with the compressed presentation file and then click Next. If you didn't install this feature when you installed Freelance Graphics, you're prompted to do so now.

6. Click Finish to close the Save and Go - Finish dialog box and allow Freelance Graphics to begin compressing your presentation. When this process is complete, you see the Save and Go dialog box. Read the information to find out how to run the compressed file and then click Yes to create another copy of the file or No if you don't want another copy.

Special Effects

If you plan to run your presentation as a screen show, you can use transitions (visual effects), sound, and timing to make the transitions between pages much more dramatic and interesting to the viewer. This can help prevent people from nodding off during your presentation! Be careful not to add *too* many special effects to your presentation, though — you don't want these effects to distract from the content of your presentation.

Adding sound effects

Follow these steps to attach a sound effect to a page of your presentation:

1. Display the page you want to attach the sound to, and then choose Page⇨Screen Show Effects. The Page Properties InfoBox appears.

2. Click the Screen Show tab of the InfoBox and select the sound from the Sound drop-down list (or click the Browse button to find another sound elsewhere on your system).

3. For additional sound options, click the Options button, select the desired options, and then click OK. Click the Close button of the InfoBox.

4. Choose Presentation⇨Run Screen Show⇨From Current Page to run the show and hear the sound effects. Repeat these steps if you want to switch to a different sound effect.

To remove a sound effect, choose Page⇨Screen Show Effects, and then select [No Sound] from the Sound drop-down list.

See also "Running a screen show," earlier in this part.

Adding transitions

Transitions are the visual effects that appear when you move from one page to the next in a screen show. Freelance Graphics provides dozens of transitions (such as curtains, dissolve, and paintbrush) for moving between pages in a screen show. You can set a visual effect for each page separately or assign a single visual effect to every page in a presentation.

To add a transition to one page, follow these steps:

1. Display the page and then choose Page⇨Screen Show Effects. The Page Properties InfoBox appears.

 2. On the Screen Show tab of the InfoBox, select a transition from the list box. Click the Close button of the InfoBox.

3. Choose <u>P</u>resentation⇨<u>R</u>un Screen Show⇨From <u>C</u>urrent Page to run the show and view the transition. Repeat these steps if you want to switch to a different visual effect.

To add a transition to all the pages in a presentation, follow these steps:

1. Choose <u>P</u>resentation⇨<u>S</u>et Up Screen Show. The Set Up Screen Show dialog box appears.

2. In the Apply To area of the Page Effects tab, select whether you want to apply the visual effect to All <u>E</u>xisting Pages or to <u>N</u>ew Pages only.

3. In the <u>T</u>ransition list, select the visual effect you want to use.

 4. Click OK, and then choose <u>P</u>resentation⇨<u>R</u>un Screen Show⇨ From <u>B</u>eginning to run the show and view the visual effects. Repeat these steps if you want to switch to a different transition.

See also "Running a screen show," earlier in this part.

Timing your pages

You can set a presentation page to advance to the next page, either manually or automatically.

To change the timing of one page, follow these steps:

1. Display the page and then choose Pa<u>g</u>e⇨Screen Sho<u>w</u> Effects. The Page Properties InfoBox appears.

2. In the Advance To Next Page area of the Screen Show tab, select one of the following options:

- Trigger Manually (Click or Keypress)

- Trigger Automatically, After *n* Sec. (type the number of seconds that you want this page to remain on-screen before Freelance Graphics displays the next page)

3. Click the Close button of the InfoBox.

 4. Choose Presentation⇨Run Screen Show⇨From Current Page to test the timings. Repeat these steps if you need to adjust the timings.

To change the timing of all pages in a presentation, follow these steps:

1. Choose Presentation⇨Set Up Screen Show. The Set Up Screen Show dialog box appears.

2. In the Display Next Page area of the Page Effects tab, select one of the following options:

- On Click or Keypress

- After *n* Seconds (type the number of seconds that you want this page to remain on-screen before Freelance Graphics displays the next page)

3. Click OK to close the dialog box.

 4. Choose Presentation⇨Run Screen Show⇨From Beginning to test the timings. Repeat these steps if you need to adjust the timings.

See also "Running a screen show," earlier in this part.

Views

Freelance Graphics provides three views that allow you to see your work in different ways: Current Page view, Page Sorter view, and Outliner view. To switch among the different views, click the tabs that appear near the top of the Freelance Graphics window — just under the SmartIcons. Following are brief descriptions of these views:

✦ Current Page view displays a presentation one page at a time.

✦ Page Sorter view provides thumbnail sketches of all the pages in a presentation.

✦ Outliner view displays the text from your presentation pages using an outline format.

Current Page view

To work in Current Page view, click the Current Page tab. Use this view when you want to work with the text and graphics in your presentation one page at a time. When creating a presentation, you'll probably display this view most often. This view includes buttons that allow you to quickly add a new page, insert clip art, add speaker notes, and access the drawing tools. When you use a SmartMaster content topic, a Content Advice button is also available.

 To move between pages in the Current Page view, use the Page Number button near the right end of the status bar. The left and right arrow buttons that appear on either side of this button enable you to move to the previous page or next page, respectively. You also can press PgUp and PgDn to move between pages.

Outliner view

To work in Outliner view, click the Outliner tab. As you might expect, Outliner view displays the text of your pages in an outline format, with text indented at various levels. Thumbnail sketches of the pages appear along the left side of the Outliner view. This view also displays the page number, page title, and text from bulleted lists and "Click here..." text blocks. You can use this view to quickly enter the text for a new presentation or to reorganize existing text in a presentation. Experiment with the buttons at the top of the Outliner tab to see the different features or views available on the Outliner tab.

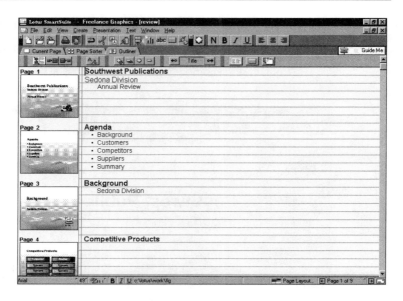

 From the Outliner view, you can quickly move to a specific page in Current Page view by double-clicking the page icon or thumbnail sketch.

Page Sorter view

To work in the Page Sorter view, click the Page Sorter tab. This view provides an overall view of the pages in your presentation. You see a thumbnail sketch of each page, along with the number and title of each page. Use the scroll bars to view additional pages, if necessary. To see a larger version of the sketches, choose View⇨Zoom⇨In. Choose View⇨Zoom⇨Out to see a smaller view of the thumbnail sketches (with more displayed on-screen). If you need to rearrange or copy pages in your presentation, use this view. To delete a page, select it and press the Delete key.

 Choose File⇨Copy Pages from Other Files if you want to copy a page from another presentation. If the copied page uses a different SmartMaster, the SmartMaster in the current presentation replaces it.

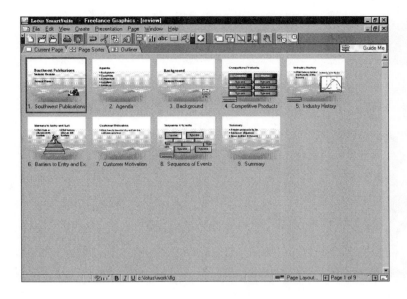

 TIP

From the Page Sorter view, you can double-click the thumbnail sketch to quickly move to that page in Current Page view.

See also "Changing the page order," earlier in this part.

Part VI

Approach

Approach is a powerful database manager that is included with Lotus SmartSuite Millennium Edition. Use Approach to create databases that help you store, manage, organize, manipulate, and create reports of your data. Database applications like Approach are typically more complex and difficult to understand and use than other applications (such as spreadsheets or word processors), but this Part gives you all the steps that you need to use Approach with confidence. Keep in mind that if your goal is simply to create a short list or table of data that you can summarize, sort, and print, you may choose to enter your data in a 1-2-3 worksheet instead of in Approach. (If that's the case, see Part III.)

This part gets you started on the basics of Approach, or reminds you how to perform common Approach tasks if you've used the program before. For much more detail on using Approach than what you find here, get your hands on a copy of *Lotus SmartSuite Millennium Edition For Dummies,* by Michael Meadhra and Jan Weingarten (published by IDG Books Worldwide, Inc.).

In this part . . .

- ✔ **Creating a new database from scratch**
- ✔ **Creating a new database by using SmartMasters**
- ✔ **Entering and editing data in your database**
- ✔ **Finding data in your database**
- ✔ **Modifying and printing reports**
- ✔ **Sorting database records**

Creating a Database

Approach enables you to work with many database file types (such as dBASE, Paradox, and FoxPro), without requiring that these other database programs be installed on your computer. When you're ready to create a new database in Approach, you have the following three options:

✦ Create a blank database and define your own fields.

✦ Create a database form based on a *SmartMaster template*. Approach includes 51 different SmartMaster templates for forms (such as Accounts, Employees, and Household Inventory).

✦ Create an automated database application based on a *SmartMaster application*. Approach provides 12 SmartMaster applications (such as Checkbook Register, Loan Amortization, and Invoice and Order Tracking). Some of the SmartMaster applications are installed automatically using the typical (default) install process. To install the additional SmartMaster applications, run a custom install and select the options that you want to install.

An Approach database includes two different views of your data — the Form view and the Worksheet view. The Form view displays one record at a time, with all fields displayed on-screen (in a fill-in-the-blanks format). The Worksheet view displays multiple records in a tablelike format, but you may not see all the fields on-screen at one time. Click the tabs near the top of the Approach window to switch between the two views.

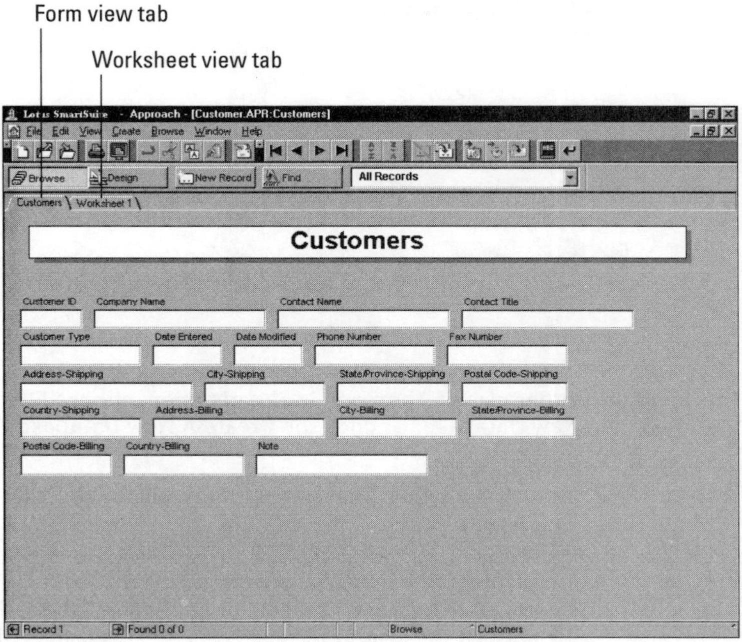

Form view tab

Worksheet view tab

Creating a blank database

To save time and frustration, you should always try to begin your database by using one of the SmartMasters provided with Approach. (Refer to the next two sections in this part.) However, if none of the SmartMasters fit your specific application, you can create a blank database from scratch.

Follow these steps to create a blank database:

1. If you see the Welcome to Lotus Approach dialog box on-screen, click the Create A New File Using A SmartMaster tab (even though you won't be using a SmartMaster in this procedure).

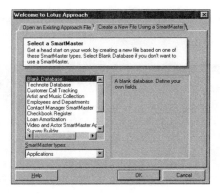

 Otherwise, if Approach is already open, choose File⇨ New Database (or click the Create A New Database File SmartIcon).

2. In the list of SmartMaster templates, select Blank Database.

3. Click OK. The New dialog box appears.

4. In the File Name text box, type a name for the file. In most cases you should use the default file type — dBASE IV (*.DBF). If you need to use another file type, however, select it from the Create Type drop-down list.

5. Click Create. The Creating New Database dialog box appears.

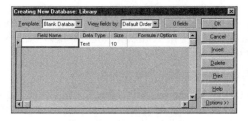

6. Specify the field names, data types, and field sizes for each field in the new database. (Press Tab after each item to move to the next box.) If you need help with this step, click the Help button in the dialog box. Click the Options button if you want to specify default values or validation options.

At this point, you can change your mind and decide to use ready-made fields from an existing Approach template. To do so, select the template name from the Template drop-down list.

7. When you're finished, click OK. Approach creates and then displays the database. Now you are ready to begin entering data in the database.

See also "Entering and Editing Data," later in this part.

To insert new fields after you've already created a database, choose Create⇔Field Definition. In the Field Definition dialog box, click the Insert button, specify the field information, and then click OK. You also can use this dialog box to modify existing field definitions.

Creating a database application based on a SmartMaster

The SmartMaster applications feature point-and-click access to different areas of an automated database. If you want to create a database form based on a SmartMaster template, rather than a full-blown application, skip to the next section. You can access the SmartMaster applications from the Welcome to Lotus Approach dialog box that appears when you start Approach, or from the New dialog box.

To create a database based on a SmartMaster application, follow these steps:

1. If you see the Welcome to Lotus Approach dialog box on-screen, click the Create A New File Using A SmartMaster tab.

Otherwise, if Approach is already open, choose File⇔ New Database (or click the Create A New Database File SmartIcon).

2. In the SmartMaster Types drop-down list, select Applications.

3. In the list of SmartMaster applications, select the application that you want to use. A description of the selected application appears in a gray box to the right of the list, as shown in the following figure.

4. Click OK. The application that you selected appears on-screen.

Creating a database form based on a SmartMaster

The SmartMaster templates provide ready-made forms that you can use to immediately begin entering data. You can access the SmartMaster templates from the Welcome to Lotus Approach dialog box that appears when you start Approach, or from the New dialog box.

To create a database form based on a SmartMaster template, follow these steps:

1. If you see the Welcome To Lotus Approach dialog box on-screen, click the Create A New File Using A SmartMaster tab.

Otherwise, if Approach is already open, choose File⇨ New Database (or click the Create A New Database File SmartIcon).

2. In the SmartMaster Types drop-down list, select Templates.

3. In the list of SmartMaster templates, select the template that you want to use. A description of the selected template appears in a gray box to the right of the list, as shown in the following figure.

4. Click OK. The New dialog box appears.

5. In the File Name text box, type a name for the file (or accept the default name that appears).

In most cases, you should use the default file type — dBASE IV (*.DBF). If you need to use another file type, however, select it from the Create Type drop-down list.

6. Click C<u>r</u>eate. The template that you selected appears on-screen. The following figure shows the Friends and Family template.

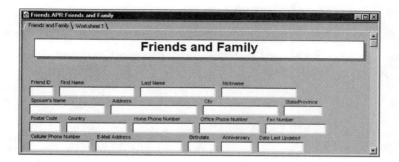

 Use the Form Assistant to add a new form to your database. Choose <u>C</u>reate⇨<u>F</u>orm and then follow the instructions provided with the Form Assistant. Click the Help button in the Form Assistant dialog box for additional information.

Opening databases created in other applications

You can open and modify databases that were created in other applications. The changes that you make to the database are saved in the original file, using the original file's format.

Use the following steps to open a database that was created in another application:

1. Choose <u>F</u>ile⇨<u>O</u>pen (or click the Open A File SmartIcon).

2. In the Files Of <u>T</u>ype drop-down list, select the file type of the database that you want to open.

3. Use the Look <u>I</u>n drop-down list to specify the drive and folder containing the file. Then click the file name to select it.

4. If you want to open the database file only for viewing, select the Open As <u>R</u>ead-Only check box.

5. Click <u>O</u>pen to open the database file.

Creating and Printing Reports

Approach includes several predesigned report layouts that you can use to organize and print data from your database. You choose which fields you want to include in the report, how you want the information presented, which records you want to group (if any), and whether you want to include totals or summary information.

The Report Assistant walks you through the process of setting up a report. After you create the report, you can then modify, preview, and print the report.

Creating a report

To use the Report Assistant to create a report, follow these steps:

1. Choose Create⇨Report. The Report Assistant dialog box appears.

2. In the View Name & Title text box, type a name for the report or accept the default name. This name will appear in the report header.

3. In the Layout list box, select the report layout that you want to use. A sample of the selected report layout appears in the dialog box.

4. In the Style drop-down list, select the style that you want to use in the report. The Sample Report panel of the dialog box reflects your selection.

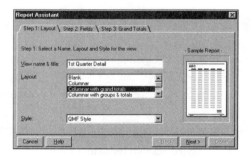

5. Click the Next button to continue.

6. In the Fields list, select the fields that you want to include in the report. Hold down the Ctrl key to select multiple fields.

7. Click the Add button to add the selected fields to the Fields To Place On View list box. To remove a field from this list box, select it and then click the Remove button.

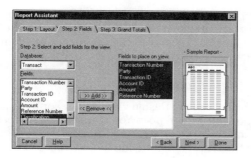

If you chose the Summary Only layout *or* the Columnar With Groups & Totals layout in Step 3 of this procedure, click the Add button to add selected fields to the Group Fields list box. In the Group By drop-down list, select how you want to group the items.

If you chose any report layout in Step 3 that uses totals or summary information, click the Next button and continue with Step 8. Otherwise, skip to Step 11.

8. In the Fields list, select the fields that you want to summarize in the report. Hold down the Ctrl key to select multiple fields.

9. Click the Add button to add the selected fields to the Summary Fields list box. To remove a field from this list box, select it and then click the Remove button.

10. In the Calculate The drop-down list, select the type of calculation that you want to perform (such as Count, Sum, or Average).

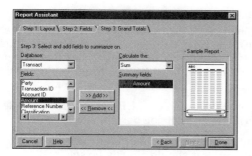

11. Click the Done button. The report appears in Design view.

If you've added totals or group names to a report but you don't see them on-screen, press Ctrl+D to switch to Design view. Then choose <u>V</u>iew⇨S<u>h</u>ow Data. You also can see the totals when you preview the report.

Modifying the layout

While displaying a report in Design view, several options are available for modifying the report. You can add fields, create charts, move and resize columns, move and delete report panels, and more. Use the Help system to find the information on the specific topic that you need:

1. Choose <u>H</u>elp⇨<u>H</u>elp Topics.

2. Click the Contents tab in the Help Topics dialog box.

3. Double-click the Top 10 Tasks topic and then double-click the Creating Reports subtopic.

4. Double-click the Revising Reports subtopic, select the topic that you want, and click <u>D</u>isplay.

5. Close the Help window when you're done.

You can easily add dates, times, or page numbers to your report. In Design view, select a panel in the report (such as Header or Body) and choose <u>P</u>anel⇨<u>I</u>nsert; then select Today's <u>D</u>ate, Current <u>T</u>ime, or <u>P</u>age Number from the resulting menu. Drag the item to the location where you want it to appear in the report.

Previewing and printing a report

To preview and print a report that you've created, follow these steps:

1. Choose <u>F</u>ile⇨<u>P</u>rint Preview (or click the Print Preview SmartIcon). The report appears in Preview mode. Click the left mouse button to magnify the display; click the right mouse button to zoom out on the display. When you're finished previewing, choose <u>F</u>ile⇨<u>P</u>rint Preview again.

2. Choose <u>F</u>ile⇨<u>P</u>rint (or click the Print The Current Selection SmartIcon). The Print dialog box appears.

3. In the Printer area, select the printer that you want to use. Your default printer should already be selected.

4. In the Print Pages area, select what you want to print: <u>A</u>ll Pages, C<u>u</u>rrent Page, or Pa<u>g</u>es. If you choose Pa<u>g</u>es, type the range of page numbers in the <u>F</u>rom and <u>T</u>o text boxes.

5. In the Copies area, select the Number Of <u>C</u>opies that you want to print and indicate whether you want to Co<u>l</u>late them.

6. Click Print to begin printing.

Most often, you'll probably want to print a single copy of the current report to the default printer. In that case, just click the Print SmartIcon and then click the Print button in the Print dialog box.

Entering and Editing Data

After you've created a database, you can begin entering data. You may find it easier to enter data by using the Form view rather than Worksheet view because Form view displays the entire contents of a record on-screen at one time.

To enter, edit, or delete data, you must be in Browse mode. If necessary, click the Browse button in the Action bar to switch to Browse mode (or press Ctrl+B).

To enter data in a database, follow these steps:

1. Display the database in Form view or Worksheet view (using the tabs below the Action bar), depending on your preference.

2. Click inside the first field of the record to select the field.

3. Enter the data that you want to display in the field.

4. Press Tab to move to the next field. If you see a warning dialog box, you've probably typed the wrong data type in a field. Correct the entry and then press Tab.

5. Repeat Steps 3 and 4 until you've entered all the data for the current record.

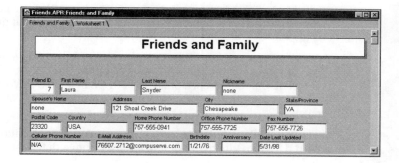

6. After you enter data for the last field, press Tab to display a new blank record. You also can click the New Record button in the Action bar to immediately display a new blank record.

The current record number appears in the Record button, near the left end of the status bar. Approach saves the previous record to your hard drive automatically.

7. When you're finished entering data in the last record, click the Enter The Record SmartIcon. Then click the form's Close button (X) to close the form.

To edit data in existing records of your database, use the navigation SmartIcons to display the record containing the data that you want to edit. Then click inside the field, edit the data, and press Enter. The navigation SmartIcons are listed in the following table:

SmartIcon	Action
	Displays the first record in the database
	Displays the previous record in the database
▶	Displays the next record in the database
	Displays the last record in the database

To duplicate a record, display the record in Form view (or click in any field of the record in Worksheet view). Then click the Duplicate Current Record SmartIcon. The new record is added to the database.

To check the spelling in a database, click the Check Spelling SmartIcon or press Ctrl+F2. Select the options that you want in the Spell Check dialog box and then click OK to begin the spell-check. Correct any misspellings and then click OK when the final dialog box appears.

To delete a record from your database, display the record in Form view (or select the record in Worksheet view). Then click the Delete The Current Record SmartIcon or press Ctrl+Del. When the warning dialog box appears, click Yes to permanently delete the record.

Be careful when deleting records, because you cannot undo the record deletion. When you delete records from a database, they're gone!

Finding Records

Approach provides several different ways to find specific records in your database — some more complex than others. This section shows you the easiest method, which uses the Find Assistant to guide you through the process.

Follow these steps to use the Find Assistant to locate the records that you want:

1. Display the database and then ensure that All Records is selected in the drop-down list in the Action bar. (If it isn't selected, select it from the list or press Ctrl+A.)

2. Click the Find button in the Action bar. A blank record appears.

3. Click the Find Assistant button in the Action bar. The Find/ Sort Assistant dialog box appears.

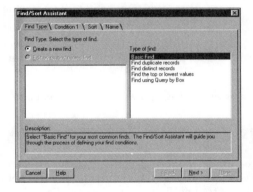

4. On the Find Type tab, select the Create A New Find option button.

5. In the Type Of Find list box, select the type of find that you want to use. In most cases, you select Basic Find from the list. Click the Next button to continue.

6. In the Fields list of the Condition 1 tab, select a field containing data that you want to find; in the Operator list, select the condition for the data; in the Values box, type the data that you want to find. (If you need help with this step, click the Help button in the Find/Sort Assistant dialog box.)

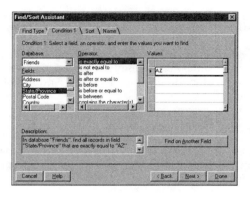

7. Click the <u>D</u>one button. If Approach found any records, they now appear on-screen.

8. Use the navigation SmartIcons to move among the found records. The Found button in the status bar displays the number of records that were found and indicates which record is currently displayed or selected.

9. To display all the records in the database again, select All Records from the drop-down list in the Action bar (or press Ctrl+A).

See also "Entering and Editing Data," earlier in this part.

Sorting Records

You can sort records in an Approach database by using one or more fields. If you want to sort the records on a single field, you can use SmartIcons to quickly perform the sort. If the field on which you want to sort includes several duplicate entries, you may want to sort the records by using multiple fields. For example, if you want to sort on Company Name and several contacts are from the same company, you may want to sort first on Company Name and then on Last Name.

Follow these steps to sort records on a single field:

1. Click the Browse button in the Action bar, if it isn't already selected. Then click the Worksheet 1 tab to display the database in Worksheet view.

2. Click the field name on which you want to sort.

3. To sort the records in ascending order on the selected field, click the Sort Field In Ascending Order SmartIcon.

To sort the records in descending order on the selected field, click the Sort Field In Descending Order SmartIcon.

To perform a sort by using multiple fields, follow these steps:

1. Click the Browse button in the Action bar, if it isn't already selected. Then click the Worksheet 1 tab to display the database in Worksheet view.

2. Choose Worksheet⇨Sort⇨Define (or press Ctrl+T). The Sort dialog box appears.

3. In the Fields list, select the field name on which you want to sort. Click the Add button.

4. In the Fields To Sort On list box, select the field you chose in Step 3. Then select either Ascending or Descending in the Sort Order drop-down list.

5. Repeat Steps 3 and 4 for each additional field in the sort.

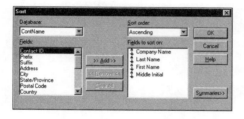

6. Click OK to perform the sort.

You don't have to perform a sort on an entire database; you can sort on just those records displayed following a find operation. To do so, perform the find (see "Finding Records" earlier in this part) and then follow the preceding steps to sort the found records. To return a database to its original sort order, press Ctrl+A.

Part VII

Organizer

Is your pocket planner becoming unwieldy? Do stick-on notes obstruct your computer screen? Maybe you are one of those people with a trashed office who *claims* to know where everything is. (You *do* know that no one believes you, right?) If any of this sounds vaguely familiar (or even if it doesn't), you need Lotus Organizer! Of course, you can't get organized overnight. This will take *some* effort on your part, but the time spent is well worth the effort. In this part, you discover how to use Organizer to help manage your time and accomplish tasks. Specific features covered here include the calendar, contacts, and to-do lists.

In this part . . .

- ✔ **Keeping track of appointments and events**
- ✔ **Creating and updating address records and phone call entries**
- ✔ **Managing your tasks with to-do lists**

Calendar

The calendar is the primary function of Organizer. With the calendar, you can manage your schedule by tracking appointments and events. You can quickly create, reschedule, and edit your appointments. The calendar also enables you to repeat appointments (useful for weekly meetings), find the next opening for an appointment, display a warning message for conflicting appointments, assign appointments to categories, and even set an alarm to remind you of an upcoming meeting, appointment, or phone call!

 You can display events such as birthdays and anniversaries in your calendar. Click the Create An Anniversary SmartIcon (or use the Anniversary section of the Organizer) to enter these events.

 If you want to schedule events that last multiple days (such as conferences, business trips, and vacations), use the Planner section of the Organizer. Click the Create A Planner Event SmartIcon to enter these events.

Changing the Calendar view

You can look at your calendar by using four different views: Day per Page, Work Week, Week per Page, and Month. Each view displays the same information but in a different format. With the click of a button, you can switch to a different view. You'll probably use the Day per Page view on a daily basis, for example, and then occasionally look at the Work Week view or Month view to get a bird's-eye view of your schedule. You can schedule and edit appointments from any of the four views:

 ✦ The Day per Page view displays one day on each page.

 ✦ The Work Week view displays one week on two pages.

 ✦ The Week per Page view displays one week on a single page.

 ✦ The Month view displays an entire month on two pages.

The Toolbox appears on the left side of the Organizer screen. To switch to a different Calendar view, click one of the Calendar view icons in the Toolbox. Point to an icon and pause to see the Help bubble description. The following figure shows the Day per Page view in Calendar.

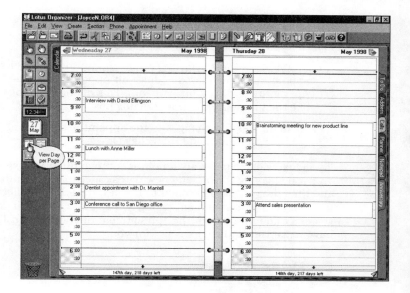

To move to another page in any of the Calendar views, click the
page turners at the bottom left and bottom right of the calendar.

To change the default Calendar view that appears when you start
Organizer, choose View⇨Calendar Preferences. Then select the
view that you want from the View area of the Calendar Preferences
dialog box.

If you're in another section of Organizer, click the Calendar tab to
switch to the Calendar section. Organizer displays the current
year with today's date outlined in red. Double-click the date that
you want and then click one of the Calendar view icons in the
Toolbox if you want to switch to a different Calendar view.

Editing appointments

Follow these steps to edit an existing appointment:

1. Double-click the start time for the appointment; or select the appointment and choose Edit⇨Edit Appointment. The Edit Appointment dialog box appears. This dialog box looks just like the Create Appointment dialog box.

2. Make the desired changes to the appointment (such as Date, Time, or Duration) and then click OK.

If you just want to move an appointment to another day, switch to a view displaying the old and new dates (such as the Month view) and then drag the appointment to the new date. If a conflict arises, the Conflicting Appointment dialog box appears, in which you can select a different time for the appointment or choose Find Time to have Organizer find an open slot for you.

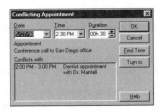

To edit the time, duration, or description for an appointment, select the appointment and then click the description. Use the time tracker that appears, if you want to edit the times.

See also "Scheduling appointments," later in this part.

Scheduling appointments

To enter an appointment in your calendar, follow these steps:

1. If you aren't already in the Calendar, click the Calendar tab and then double-click the date of the appointment.

2. Double-click the day in which you want to enter the appointment (or click the Create An Appointment SmartIcon). The Create Appointment dialog box appears.

3. If necessary, use the Date option to change the date for the appointment.

4. To specify a begin and end time for the appointment, click the Time drop-down arrow to display the time tracker. Then perform one or more of the following actions and click outside the time tracker to close it:

• Drag the top clock to change the start time for the appointment. The displayed time changes in five-minute increments.

• Drag the bottom clock to change the end time for the appointment. The displayed time changes in five-minute increments.

• To move the entire appointment (both start and end times, without changing the duration), drag the center bar in the time tracker to the new location.

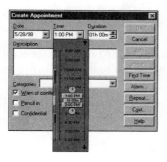

5. If necessary, use the + (plus) or – (minus) buttons beside the Duration text box to adjust the duration of the appointment.

6. In the Description text box, type the name of the appointment. You must enter a description to create an appointment.

7. Select any other options that you want to set for the current appointment. If you want to set an alarm to remind you of an upcoming meeting or appointment, click the Alarm button, select the options that you want in the Alarm dialog box, and then click OK.

8. If you want to create another appointment, click the Add button and then repeat Steps 3 through 7.

9. Click OK when you're finished. The appointments that you created now appear in the Calendar section.

You can ask Organizer to automatically repeat tasks (such as a weekly status meeting) so that you don't have to type the same information more than once! Use Steps 1 through 9 in this section to enter the first occurrence of the task. Then click the Repeat button in the Create Appointment dialog box, specify the repeat options, and click OK.

Contacts

You use the Address section of Organizer to enter all your business and personal contact information. The Address section resembles a paper address book but provides much more flexibility. You can view and print your address information by using several different layouts, for example. You also can duplicate portions of an address record so that you don't have to retype the same information (such as a company address) in multiple records.

Adding contacts

You can enter both business and home contact information in the Address book. Follow these steps to create an address record:

1. Click the Address tab and then double-click the Address page (or click the Create An Address Record SmartIcon). The Create Address dialog box appears.

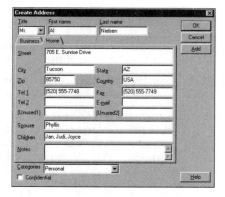

2. Click the Business tab to enter business contact information, or click the Home tab to enter personal or family contact information. (You can enter both business and personal information for a single contact.)

3. Use the Title, First Name, and Last Name text boxes to enter the name of the contact.

4. Use the remaining text boxes in the Create Address dialog box to enter all available information that you want to list in the address record.

5. If you want to create another address record, click the Add button and then repeat Steps 2 through 4.

6. Click OK when you're finished. The address records that you created now appear in the Address section — listed under the tab letter that corresponds to the first letter of the contact's last name.

 If you want to dial phone calls from Organizer by using the phone numbers listed in the Address section, use parentheses to surround the area code of the phone number, such as (555) 555-5555.

Changing the Address view

You can view the address records in four different ways. Each view displays some or all of the information supplied when you created the address records. The four views are described below:

 ✦ The View All icon displays all the available information.

 ✦ The View Address icon displays the name, job title, company name, address, phone number, and fax number.

 ✦ The View Contact icon displays the name, phone numbers, fax number, and e-mail address.

 ✦ The View Phone icon displays only the name and primary phone number.

To switch to a different Address view, click one of the Address view icons in the Toolbox (on the left side of the screen). Point to an icon and pause to see the Help bubble description. To move to another page, click the letter tabs in the Address section to display the page you want.

 To change the default address view that appears when you start Organizer, choose View⇨Address Preferences. Then select the view that you want from the View area of the Address Preferences dialog box.

Editing contacts

To edit an existing contact in the Address section, follow these steps:

1. Display the address record by clicking the tab letter that corresponds to the first letter of the contact's last name. (If someone's last name is Smith, for example, click the "S" tab.)

2. Double-click the address record; or select the record and choose Edit⇨Edit Address. The Edit Address dialog box appears. This dialog box closely resembles the Create Address dialog box.

3. Make the desired changes to the address record and then click OK.

Setting up phone calls

You can use the Calls section in Organizer to track the status of your incoming and outgoing phone calls and to schedule upcoming calls. To add a call entry to the Calls section, follow these steps:

1. Click the Calls tab and then double-click the Calls page (or click the Create A Calls Entry SmartIcon). The Create Call dialog box appears.

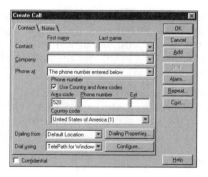

2. Type the contact's First Name, Last Name, and Company. If you've already entered the contact in the Address section, you can select the Last Name and Company from the drop-down lists.

3. Specify the phone number and dialing options that you want to use.

If you want to set an alarm to remind you of an upcoming call, click the Alarm button, select the options that you want in the Alarm dialog box, and then click OK.

4. Click the Notes tab in the Create Call dialog box.

5. Specify the Date and Time for the call in the appropriate text boxes. Organizer later supplies the Duration, based on the length of the call.

6. In the Notes text box, type a description for the call entry.

7. Select any other options that you want to set for the call. If you want to create another call entry, click the Add button and then repeat Steps 2 through 6.

8. Click OK when you're finished. The call entries that you created now appear in the Calls section.

To move to another page, click the letter tabs in the Calls section to display the page that you want.

 To change the preferences for the Calls section in Organizer, choose View⇨Calls Preferences. Select or change the dialog box options as desired and then click OK.

Printing Organizer Data

You can print information from any section of Organizer, using a variety of different print layouts. To print Organizer data, follow these steps:

 1. Choose File⇨Print (or click the Print SmartIcon). The Print dialog box appears.

2. In the Section drop-down list, select the section containing data that you want to print, if it isn't already selected.

3. In the Layout drop-down list, select how you want the printed information to appear.

4. Click the Layouts button to see a preview of the selected layout in the Layouts dialog box, and then make additional adjustments if necessary. Use the Preferences options in the Layouts dialog box to specify the information that you want to print.

If you print a Monthly calendar, for example, you may want to switch to the Landscape print orientation. Click OK to return to the Print dialog box.

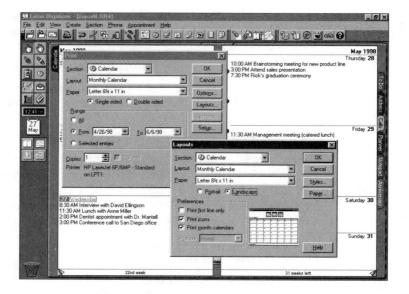

5. Select the paper size and type from the Paper drop-down list.

6. Click the Single Sided option button or the Double Sided option button.

7. In the Range area, select the option specifying the range of information that you want to print.

8. In the Copies box, type the number of copies that you want to print. If you choose more than one copy and you want to print the copies in sequence, select the Collated check box.

9. Click OK to begin printing.

When you print address records, the order in which your records are printed is based on the sort order. To change the sort order before you print, choose the View menu and then select from the following options: By Last Name (which is the default), By Company, By Zip, and Category.

To-Do Lists

Organizer provides a To Do section that helps you track the tasks that you need to accomplish. You can group, prioritize, sort, and print your tasks. As an option, you also can specify the start and due date for each task and display the To Do tasks in the Calendar section.

If you want to keep track of lists, notes, memos, spreadsheets, charts, and other items that don't fit anywhere else in Organizer, use the Notepad section. You can type the information into the Notepad or import data from existing files. To access the Notepad section, click the Create A Notepad Page SmartIcon.

Adding tasks

Follow these steps to add a task in the To Do section:

 1. Click the To Do tab and then double-click the To Do page (or click the Create A To Do Task SmartIcon). The Create Task dialog box appears.

2. Type a description for the To Do task in the Description text box.

3. Select any other options that you want to set for the task.

If you specify dates for the task and you want to set an alarm, click the Alarm button, select the options that you want in the Alarm dialog box, and then click OK.

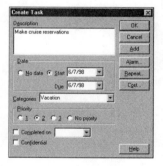

4. If you want to add another task, click the Add button and then repeat Steps 2 and 3.

5. Click OK when you're finished. The tasks that you added now appear in the To Do section.

Completing a task

After you finish a task in the To Do section, you can mark the task as completed. Display the page containing the To Do item and click the gray box beside the task. A green check mark appears beside the task. Click the check mark if you need to remove it.

Editing tasks

If you want to edit the wording of a task, follow these steps:

1. In the To Do section, double-click the To Do task that you want to edit; or select the task and choose Edit⇨Edit Task.

2. Make the desired changes to the To Do task in the Edit Task dialog box and then click OK.

To change the preferences for the To Do section in Organizer, choose View⇨To Do Preferences. Select or change the options in the To Do Preferences dialog box as desired and then click OK.

Part VIII

Sharing Information among SmartSuite Applications

One of the major benefits of using Windows applications is that you can easily share and link data between the applications. Lotus SmartSuite Millennium Edition takes this concept a giant step further by providing applications that truly work *together*, because they all use similar interfaces and features. (Now you know why they call it *SmartSuite!*) After you find out how to use one of the SmartSuite applications, you can get up to speed more quickly in the other SmartSuite applications.

This part shows you how to exchange information between SmartSuite applications. For example, you find out how to bring 1-2-3 worksheet data into a Word Pro document so that you don't need to insert a table and retype the information.

In this part . . .

- ✔ Using the Clipboard for simple copy and paste operations
- ✔ Linking and embedding data between applications
- ✔ Sharing data between two specific SmartSuite applications

Copying and Pasting with the Clipboard

The *Clipboard* is a temporary storage area into which you can copy or move data from a Windows application. You can then paste this information from the Clipboard into another Windows application. When you copy or move data within a single application, such as 1-2-3, you also use the Clipboard. The Clipboard can hold only one object at a time. The data you copy or move is called the *source;* the new location of the pasted data is called the *destination.*

 To switch between open Windows applications, click the application buttons in the taskbar (or press Alt+Tab).

Use the following steps to copy data from one SmartSuite application to another:

1. In the source application, select the text or object that you want to copy.

 2. Choose Edit⇨Copy or click the Copy To Clipboard SmartIcon. The information you copy is placed in the Clipboard.

3. Switch to the destination application and then position the insertion point where you want the copied object to appear.

 4. Choose Edit⇨Paste or click the Paste Clipboard Contents SmartIcon.

To move, or *cut and paste,* data from one SmartSuite application to another, follow these steps:

1. In the source application, select the text or object that you want to move.

 2. Choose Edit⇨Cut or click the Cut To Clipboard SmartIcon. The information you cut is placed in the Clipboard.

3. Switch to the destination application and then position the insertion point where you want the cut object to appear.

 4. Choose Edit⇨Paste or click the Paste Clipboard Contents SmartIcon.

 You also can use keyboard shortcuts to copy, cut, and paste information between applications. Use Ctrl+C to copy data to the Clipboard or Ctrl+X to cut data to the Clipboard. Then use Ctrl+V to paste the Clipboard data into the file.

Object Linking and Embedding

Object Linking and Embedding, also referred to as OLE (pronounced *o-lay*), is a method used in Windows applications to link or embed data (also called *objects*) between applications. A link is a connection between two applications that enables the applications to share data. When you *link* data, a copy of the linked data appears in the destination application. Changes that you make to the linked data in the source file are automatically reflected in the destination file. When you *embed* data, the data becomes a part of the destination file but isn't linked to the source. To edit an embedded object, double-click the object in the destination file.

The basic steps for linking and embedding data between applications are very similar. The following procedures list these basic steps. Later in this part, you find out how to share data between different pairs of SmartSuite applications.

Embedding data

In Lotus SmartSuite, you use the Edit⇨Paste Special command to embed objects that you copy or cut from another application. If you want to embed a new object (that you create from scratch), you use the Create⇨Object command. This section shows you the methods for both types of embedding.

To embed an object from another application, follow these steps:

1. Switch to the application that contains the data you want to embed (the source) and then select the data.

 2. Choose Edit⇨Copy or click the Copy To Clipboard SmartIcon. The information that you copy is placed in the Clipboard.

3. Switch to the destination application and then position the insertion point where you want the embedded object to appear.

4. Choose Edit⇨Paste Special. The Paste Special dialog box appears.

   The following figure shows the Paste Special dialog box that appears when Word Pro is the destination. (The options that you see may differ.)

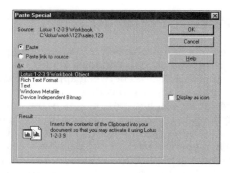

5. Click the <u>P</u>aste option button.

6. Select the format that you want to use from the <u>A</u>s list box. In most cases, you want to select the first item in the list.

7. Click OK. The embedded object appears in the destination file.

To create a new OLE object from scratch, follow these steps:

1. Switch to the application in which you want to embed the new OLE object.

2. Choose <u>C</u>reate⇨Object. The Create Object dialog box appears.

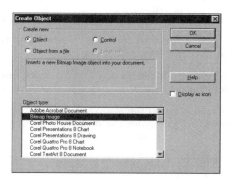

3. In the Create New area, select the <u>O</u>bject option button.

4. In the O<u>b</u>ject Type list box, select the type of OLE object that you want to create and then click OK.

5. Use the tools provided in the source application to create the object. If you chose a Bitmap file, for example, you can now draw the bitmap. Click outside the border of the object when you're done.

After you embed an object, edits that you make in the source file aren't reflected in the destination file. To edit an embedded object, double-click the object in the destination file; then use the menus, icons, and toolbars of the source application that appear. To delete an embedded object, select the object and press the Delete key.

Linking data

To link data between two applications, follow these steps:

1. Switch to the application that contains the data you want to link (the source) and then select the data.

2. Choose Edit⇨Copy or click the Copy To Clipboard SmartIcon. The information that you copy is placed in the Clipboard.

3. Switch to the destination application and then position the insertion point where you want the copied object to appear.

4. Choose Edit⇨Paste Special. The Paste Special dialog box appears.

5. Click the Paste Link To Source option button.

6. Select the format that you want to use from the As list box. In most cases, you want to use the default selection.

7. Click OK. The linked object appears in the destination file.

After you create the link, any edits that you make in the source file are automatically reflected in the destination file. To edit an object that's linked, double-click the object in the destination file. To delete a linked object, select the object and press the Delete key.

Sharing Information

This section shows you how you can get the most out of Lotus SmartSuite Millennium Edition by sharing information between two specific SmartSuite applications. When sharing data, you can copy or link information between the applications. You can link data between the applications if you want data in the destination application to update whenever changes are made to the source application. When you copy and paste data between applications, no such link exists.

These are some of the more common ways to share data in SmartSuite — there are many more possibilities, of course. For more ideas, you can refer to the SmartSuite online Help or the program documentation.

See also "Object Linking and Embedding," earlier in this part, and "Help Information," in Part II.

Sharing data between 1-2-3 and Freelance Graphics

You can share data between 1-2-3 and Freelance Graphics by copying a 1-2-3 chart or range of cells to a Freelance Graphics presentation, copying table data or a graphic from Freelance Graphics to 1-2-3, or linking a 1-2-3 range of cells to a Freelance Graphics chart.

Follow these steps to copy a 1-2-3 chart to a Freelance Graphics presentation:

1. In Freelance Graphics, open the presentation in which you want the chart to appear.

2. Click the New Page button. The New Page dialog box appears.

3. Click the Page Layouts tab, select the 1 Chart layout, and click OK.

4. Switch to 1-2-3 and display the sheet that contains the chart you want to copy.

5. Select the chart and drag it onto the Freelance Graphics button in the Windows taskbar, but don't release the mouse button.

6. When Freelance Graphics becomes active, drag the 1-2-3 chart to the Click Here To Create Chart block in the Freelance Graphics presentation.

7. Release the mouse button to drop the chart. The following figure shows a 1-2-3 chart copied to a Freelance Graphics presentation.

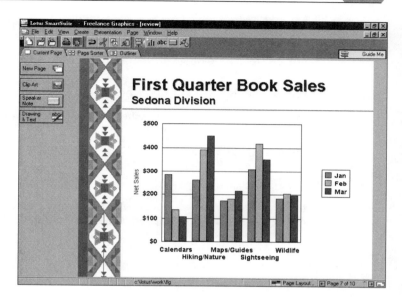

To copy a graphic from Freelance Graphics to 1-2-3, follow these steps:

1. In Freelance Graphics, open the presentation that contains the graphic you want to copy.

2. Select the graphic and then click the Copy SmartIcon. If you want to copy an entire page from your presentation (including all text and design elements), click the page in Page Sorter view and then click the Copy SmartIcon.

3. Switch to 1-2-3 and click the cell where you want the upper-left corner of the graphic to appear.

4. Click the Paste SmartIcon.

5. Move or size the graphic as necessary.

While in 1-2-3, you can double-click the graphic to edit it using Freelance Graphics. When you're done, choose File➪Exit & Return to go back to 1-2-3.

Sharing data between 1-2-3 and Word Pro

To share data between 1-2-3 and Word Pro, you can copy or link a 1-2-3 range of cells to a Word Pro document, copy data from a Word Pro table into 1-2-3, embed 1-2-3 data into Word Pro, and use 1-2-3 data for a mail merge in Word Pro.

Follow these steps to link a 1-2-3 range of cells to a Word Pro document.

1. In 1-2-3, select the range of cells that you want to link to the Word Pro document.

2. Choose Edit➪Copy or click the Copy SmartIcon.

3. Switch to Word Pro and click where you want the linked data to appear in the document.

4. Choose Edit➪Paste Special. The Paste Special dialog box appears.

5. Select the Paste Link To Source option button.

6. In the As list box, select Lotus 1-2-3 Workbook Object and then click OK. The 1-2-3 data appears in a frame in the Word Pro document.

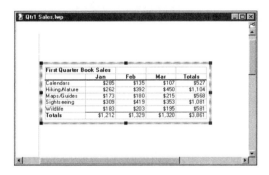

To resize the object in the Word Pro document, right-click the object and choose Frame Properties. Select the Scaling options you want from the Graphic And Watermark Options tab of the InfoBox.

After you copy a range of 1-2-3 cells to Word Pro, the object in Word Pro retains the gridlines from the workbook. If you don't want gridlines to appear in the linked object, remove the display of gridlines in 1-2-3 before you copy the workbook object. To do so, choose View➪Set View Preferences, click the View tab, and deselect the Grid Lines check box.

To copy data from a Word Pro table into 1-2-3, follow these steps:

1. In Word Pro, open the document that contains the table you want to copy, and click inside the table.

2. Choose Table➪Select➪Entire Table Contents.

3. Choose Edit⇨Copy, or click the Copy SmartIcon.

4. Switch to 1-2-3 and click the cell where you want the upper-left corner of the table to appear.

5. Choose Edit⇨Paste or click the Paste SmartIcon. The table data from Word Pro now appears in the worksheet. Each cell from the Word Pro table now occupies a separate cell in 1-2-3.

Sharing data between Word Pro and Freelance Graphics

You can share data between Word Pro and Freelance Graphics by copying a Freelance Graphics presentation page or graphic into Word Pro, or by creating a Freelance Graphics presentation from a Word Pro outline. You also can create and format a table in Word Pro and copy it to a Freelance Graphics presentation page.

To copy a graphic (or an entire page in a presentation) from Freelance Graphics to Word Pro, follow these steps:

1. In Freelance Graphics, open the presentation that contains the graphic you want to copy.

2. Select the graphic and then click the Copy SmartIcon. If you want to copy an entire page from your presentation (including all text and design elements), click the page in Page Sorter view and then click the Copy SmartIcon.

3. Switch to Word Pro and position the insertion point where you want the upper-left corner of the graphic to appear.

4. Click the Paste SmartIcon.

5. The graphic appears in a frame in the Word Pro document. Move or size the graphic, as necessary. The following figure shows two pages from a Freelance Graphics presentation pasted into a Word Pro document.

To add a border around the graphic, right-click the graphic and choose Frame Properties. Select the border options that you want from the Color, Pattern, And Line Style tab in the InfoBox. If you want to resize the graphic, adjust the Scaling settings on the Graphic And Watermark Options tab of the InfoBox.

To automatically create a Freelance Graphics presentation from a Word Pro outline, follow these steps:

1. In Word Pro, open the document containing the outline that you want to use to create the presentation.

2. Select the entire outline in the Word Pro document.

3. Choose Edit⇨Script & Macros⇨Run. The Run Script dialog box appears.

4. Select the Run Script Saved In Another File option button and then click Browse.

5. In the Files Of Type drop-down list, select Script Source (*.lss).

6. Select the file named PRSIT.LSS and then click Open.

7. Click OK to close the Run Script dialog box. The script runs, and Freelance Graphics opens and displays the outline as a presentation. Top-level outline text converts to title text in Freelance Graphics, second-level outline text converts to first-level bullet text, third-level outline text becomes second-level bullet text, and so on.

If you want to choose another look for the presentation in Freelance Graphics, choose Presentation⇨Choose a Different SmartMaster Look. Select the look that you want from the list box and then click OK.

Part IX

SmartSuite and the Web

SmartSuite Millennium Edition delivers fun and powerful new tools that help you and your team become more efficient and get the most out of the Internet. You can bring Web data into 1-2-3, for example, and maintain a connection to the source Web page that you can refresh as needed. Lotus SmartCenter now includes its own Web browser, so you can access and search for information on the Web directly from SmartCenter. In addition, you can add hyperlinks to text or objects and publish your SmartSuite documents to the Web. To use the features covered in this part, you need to have access to the Internet.

In this part . . .

✔ **Working with hyperlinks in SmartSuite documents**

✔ **Accessing the Web from SmartCenter**

✔ **Bringing data from the Web into a SmartSuite document**

✔ **Converting your SmartSuite data to Web pages**

✔ **Creating Web sites with FastSite, the document publisher**

Adding Hyperlinks to SmartSuite Documents

A *hyperlink* is a cross-reference or link that lets you jump to a Web site, another file, or an object in the current document. You can create hyperlinks in 1-2-3, Word Pro, and Freelance Graphics.

Use the following steps to create a hyperlink:

1. Select the cell, text, button, or picture for which you want to create a hyperlink.

2. Choose Create➪Hyperlink or click the Create/Edit Hyperlink SmartIcon. The Create Hyperlink dialog box appears. This dialog box varies slightly among applications; the following figure is from 1-2-3.

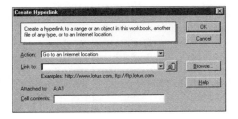

3. In the Action drop-down list, select the type of hyperlink that you want to create.

4. In the Link To drop-down list, specify the path for the hyperlink. If you want to paste a location from the Clipboard, click the Paste icon beside the Link To list.

5. If you're using 1-2-3, type the text for the hyperlink (the text that appears in the worksheet) in the Cell Contents text box. Be careful — the text that you type here overwrites the contents of the current cell.

   If you're using Word Pro, type the text for the hyperlink (the text that appears in the document) in the Linked Text text box.

   If you're creating a hyperlink for a button, the text that you type appears on the button.

6. Click OK to close the dialog box and insert the hyperlink.

7. To go to the location specified in a 1-2-3 hyperlink, click the object to which you attached the hyperlink. In Word Pro, double-click the hyperlinked text. In Freelance Graphics, run the screen show and click the text to which the hyperlink is attached.

To display the path of the hyperlink, point to the object to which you attached the hyperlink.

To edit an existing hyperlink, right-click the hyperlink, choose Edit Hyperlink from the shortcut menu, and make your desired changes in the Edit Hyperlink dialog box. To remove a hyperlink, right-click the hyperlink and choose Remove Hyperlink from the shortcut menu. The hyperlink disappears.

Bringing Web Data into SmartSuite

You can easily find information on the Web or bring actual Web data into an application without leaving SmartSuite. This section shows you how to use the new SmartCenter Browser, open HTML files in SmartSuite, view HTML source code, and open Web tables in 1-2-3.

Browsing with SmartCenter

You can make travel reservations and obtain up-to-date news, stock quotes, and weather information from the Web by using the Internet folders in SmartCenter. Because SmartCenter now has a built-in browser, you can obtain this information without having to switch to a separate Web browser application!

To access SmartCenter's Internet folders, follow these steps:

1. Establish your Internet connection.

2. Open Lotus SmartCenter, if it isn't already displayed at the top of your screen. (Click the Start button and then choose Programs⇨Lotus SmartSuite⇨Lotus SmartCenter.)

3. Click the Internet drawer in SmartCenter and select the folder that you want. Some folders (such as the News and Weather folders) require that you choose the information you want to display in the folder. If this is the case, you see instructions for how to provide the information. If you select a folder that links to the Web, you see ducks scrolling across the top of the folder while the Web page is loading.

4. To maximize the folder and display a split screen — with links in the left window and the SmartCenter Browser in the right window — click the Maximize button in the drawer. To return to the previous view, click the drawer's Restore button.

The Suite Help drawer in SmartCenter provides additional Internet access. Click the Lotus Online or SmartSuite Tips folder to obtain Help information or tips on using SmartSuite.

See also "SmartCenter" in Part II.

Opening HTML files in SmartSuite

What is HTML, you may ask? HTML stands for Hypertext Markup Language, the language that you use to write and format Web pages in SmartSuite as well as other applications. You can open existing HTML files created by you (or others), analyze or edit the files, save them, and then share them with others via the Web.

To open a file from the Internet, follow these steps:

1. Establish your Internet connection.

2. Switch to the SmartSuite application in which you want to open an Internet file.

3. Display the Internet Tools SmartIcon bar (by right-clicking any of the SmartIcons and selecting Internet Tools).

4. Click the Open File From The Internet SmartIcon. The Open from Internet dialog box appears.

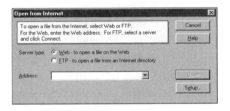

5. Select the <u>W</u>eb option button to open a file on the Web. (Or, if you want to open a file from an Internet directory, select the <u>F</u>TP option button.)

6. In the <u>A</u>ddress box, type the Web address (the URL).

7. Click the <u>O</u>pen button to open the file.

You can access many Internet features in SmartSuite directly from the Internet Tools SmartIcon bar. To display this SmartIcon bar, right-click any of the SmartIcons and select Internet Tools.

To open a local HTML file from disk, follow these steps:

1. Choose <u>F</u>ile⇨<u>O</u>pen or click the Open SmartIcon.

2. In the Files Of <u>T</u>ype drop-down list, select HTML (*.HTM*).

3. In the Look <u>I</u>n drop-down list, specify the drive and folder that contain the HTML file you want to open.

4. In the File <u>N</u>ame text box, type the name of the HTML file or select it from the list.

5. Click the <u>O</u>pen button to open the file.

Viewing HTML source code

If you want to see the HTML source codes for a document (rather than the formatting represented by the codes), follow these steps:

1. In Word Pro, choose File⇨Internet⇨HTML Import Options. The HTML Import Options dialog box opens.

2. Select the Import As Source Code check box and then click OK.

 3. Choose File⇨Open or click the Open SmartIcon.

4. In the Files Of Type drop-down list, select HTML (*.HTM*).

5. In the Look In drop-down list, specify the drive and folder that contains the HTML file you want to open.

6. In the File Name text box, type the name of the HTML file or select it from the list.

7. Click the Open button to open the file and view the source codes.

┌Internet Tools SmartIcons   Source code   Web Tools bar┐

Working with Web tables in 1-2-3

If you need to work with tables on the Web, you can open the Web table in 1-2-3. Because 1-2-3 maintains the link to the table on the Web, you can refresh the data from the Web site and update your table as needed.

To create a Web table in 1-2-3, follow these steps:

1. Establish your Internet connection.

2. Select the cell in the worksheet where you want the upper-left corner of the table to appear, and then choose File⇨ Internet⇨Get Data from Web. The Get Data from Web dialog box appears.

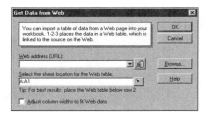

3. In the Web Address (URL) combo box, specify the Web address.

4. In the text box, type the cell or range for the Web table (or use the range selector button to select the range in the worksheet). Be sure to choose a blank area of the worksheet to avoid accidental data loss. If you preselected the cell in Step 2 of this procedure, the cell address already appears in the text box.

5. Select the Adjust Column Widths To Fit Web Data check box if you want the columns to be as wide as the information.

6. Click OK.

To refresh the data in a 1-2-3 Web table, select the Web table and then click the Refresh button in the upper-right corner of the Web table frame. If you want to refresh data for multiple Web tables at once, choose File⇨Internet⇨Refresh Web Data.

Converting SmartSuite Files to Web Pages

With SmartSuite Millennium Edition, you can easily publish documents, worksheets, presentations, and databases to the Web.

You can use Assistants and other Internet features in SmartSuite to guide you through the process of converting your SmartSuite files to Web pages.

Building a Web page in Word Pro

Although you can use other SmartSuite applications to build Web pages, Word Pro provides more Web authoring tools and formatting features that make it easy for you to create Web pages. Use these basic steps to build a Web page in Word Pro:

1. Start a new document and then select an Internet SmartMaster.

2. Double-click the divider tab, type the name of your Web page, and press Enter. If you don't see a divider tab above the document area, click the tab icon just above the vertical scroll bar. The name that you type appears in the title bar of the Web browser when a user displays your Web page.

3. Type and then format the text of your Web page. You can use the "Click here..." blocks in the SmartMaster to insert text and graphics.

4. Add any or all of the following elements, as desired: horizontal lines, links, imported pictures, and background colors or wallpaper.

5. Use a browser to preview your Web page. (Refer to the next section for details.)

6. Choose File➪Save As, specify HTML as the format in the Save As Type drop-down list, and then click OK.

7. Publish your Web page to the Internet.

If you don't have an FTP connection, you must set one up before you can publish your Web page to the Internet. For more information, search on "FTP, saving documents" in the Help system in Word Pro. You may need the help of your network administrator or Internet service provider.

Exporting a Word Pro document to HTML format

Use the following steps to export a Word Pro document to HTML format:

1. Choose File➪Internet➪HTML Export Assistant. The HTML Export Assistant dialog box appears.

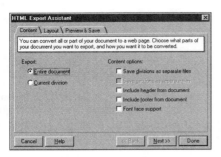

2. Select one of the following Export options: Entire Document or Current Division.

3. Select the Content options that you want to use and then click Next.

4. On the Layout tab, select the navigation options that you want and then click Next.

5. In the Saving Options area of the Preview & Save tab, select the options that you want.

6. Click the Save Locally button and then enter the requested information.

Word Pro provides Internet SmartMaster templates that include tables, graphics, forms, and backgrounds (as shown in the following figure). To access these templates in Word Pro, choose File⇨ New Document. Then click the Create From Any SmartMaster tab and select one of the Internet options in the list box. If you've already created the document, you can use the File⇨Choose Another SmartMaster command to convert the existing file to an Internet SmartMaster.

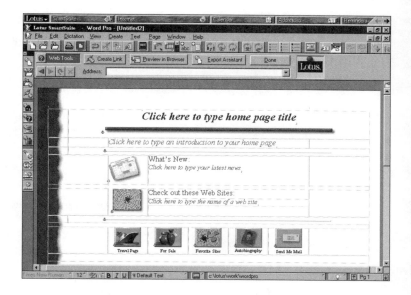

Previewing a Web page in a browser

To preview and then save your data as a Web page, follow these steps:

1. In Word Pro, choose File⇔Internet⇔Show Web Tools to display the Web Tools bar.

2. In the Web Tools bar, click the Preview In Browser button. A preview of the Web page appears in your browser.

3. Use the Windows taskbar to return to Word Pro, and click the Save button to save the file.

Saving a Freelance Graphics presentation as Web pages

Follow these steps to convert a Freelance Graphics presentation to Web pages so that you can post it as a Web presentation:

1. In Freelance Graphics, save your presentation and then choose File⇔Internet⇔Convert to Web Pages.

2. In the Convert to Web Pages - Overview dialog box, read the general instructions for this procedure and then click OK.

3. In the Web Style list box of the Convert to Web Pages - Step 1 dialog box, select the style that you want to use for your Web pages. When you select a style, a description of the style appears on the right side of the dialog box.

4. In the File Name text box, type a file name and then click Next.

5. In the Convert to Web Pages - Step 2 dialog box, select the layout options that you want and then click Next. Freelance Graphics prepares the pages for the Web presentation. (This may take a minute or so, depending on the size of your presentation.)

6. When the Convert to Web Pages - Step 3 dialog box appears, click the Preview In Browser button to view your presentation pages in a Web browser.

7. Return to Freelance Graphics. In the Convert to Web Pages - Step 3 dialog box, click the Save Locally button to save the presentation to a folder on your hard disk, and then click the Done button. The following figure shows a preview of a presentation in a browser, using the Single Image Web style (from Step 3 of this procedure).

Click here to advance page

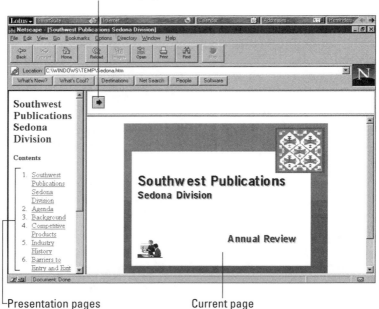

Presentation pages   Current page

Saving 1-2-3 data as an HTML table

You can convert an entire 1-2-3 workbook, the current sheet, or a range of data to an HTML table. Use the following steps to save a 1-2-3 range as an HTML table:

1. In 1-2-3, select the range that you want to save as an HTML table and then choose File⇨Internet⇨Convert to Web Pages. The Convert to Web Pages dialog box appears.

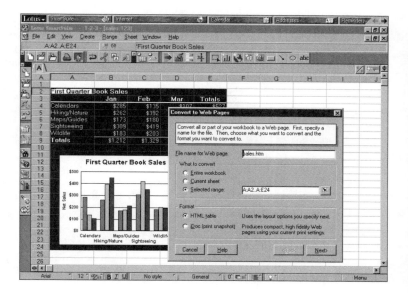

2. In the File Name For Web Page text box, type a file name for the Web page.

3. In the What To Convert area, select the Selected Range option button.

4. In the text box, type the range that you want to convert (or use the range selector button to select the range in the worksheet). If you preselected the range in Step 1 of this procedure, the range already appears in the text box.

5. In the Format area, select the HTML Table option button and then click Next.

6. Verify or change the layout options in the next dialog box and then click Next.

7. Click the Preview In Browser button to see how your page will look in the browser.

8. Use the Windows taskbar to return to 1-2-3. In the Convert To Web Pages dialog box, specify where you want to save the converted file in the Directory text box.

9. Click the Save button.

Creating Web Sites with FastSite

FastSite is a new application provided with SmartSuite Millennium
Edition that helps you create professional-looking Web sites and
publish your SmartSuite documents to the Web. This is an ideal
resource for those of us who don't quite understand HTML (and
don't want to learn!). FastSite provides dozens of SmartMasters
that you can choose from to give your Web site a cohesive and
polished look. You can customize SmartMasters for your own
organization.

Creating a Web site

FastSite walks you through the steps necessary to create a Web
site. You should create at least one of the SmartSuite files that you
want to include in your Web site before you follow these steps.
(You can add more files as necessary after you create the Web
site.) To use FastSite to create a Web site, follow these steps:

1. Click the Start button on the Windows taskbar and then
choose Programs⇨Lotus SmartSuite⇨Lotus FastSite. Alterna-
tively, you can click the SmartSuite drawer in Lotus
SmartCenter and double-click the Lotus FastSite icon in the
Lotus Applications folder. The FastSite window appears.

The left side of the FastSite window displays a site map that shows you all the components of your site and how they relate to each other. The right side of the FastSite window displays two tabbed panes: the Choose Task pane provides access to common tasks in FastSite; the Preview Web Pages pane enables you to view your Web pages and display a site from the Web.

2. On the Choose Task pane, click the Create A Site link. The Create Site - Basics dialog box appears.

3. In the Name text box, type a name for your site. This name will be used as your staging directory. (The *staging directory* stores your Web site files during the "testing" phase, until you are ready to post your site to the Internet.) You also can enter a description of your site in the Description text box, if desired.

4. Select the option button representing the conversion format that you want to use: HTML Pages or jDoc. (When you select either of these options, a description of that option appears in the dialog box.)

5. Click Next to continue. The Create Site - Web SmartMaster Look dialog box appears.

6. Select the SmartMaster look that you want to use from the list box in the upper-left corner of the dialog box. A preview of the selected look appears in the lower portion of the dialog box.

7. Click Next to continue. The Create Site - Content dialog box appears. You use this dialog box to specify which SmartSuite files you want to add to your Web site.

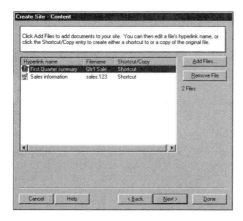

8. Click the Add Files button. In the Add Files dialog box, navigate to the drive and folder containing the files that you want to add to your Web site. Select the files and then click the Add button. Repeat this step as necessary to add more files that are located in different folders.

9. The files that you added to the site appear in a table within the Create Site - Content dialog box. To edit the name of the hyperlink, click the current hyperlink name, click the name again to get a text edit box, type the new name, and press Enter. You also can click the file's entry in the Shortcut/Copy column to toggle between creating a shortcut to the file or a copy of the file.

10. Click <u>N</u>ext to continue. FastSite displays the Create Site - Next Steps dialog box that explains what you can do next. Read this information and then click <u>D</u>one to close the dialog box.

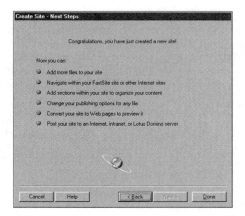

To add sections or hyperlinks to an existing site, use the Create A Section and Create A Hyperlink options on the Choose Task pane.

Editing a Web site

After you use FastSite to build a Web site, you have many options for editing the site. You can add files to a site or to a specific section within a site, change the publishing properties of a site, or select a different SmartMaster look for a site. All these editing options can be accessed directly from the Choose Task pane in the FastSite window (under the heading "Edit a Site"). Click the task that applies to your situation, make your selections or changes in the dialog box that appears, and click OK.

In addition to the editing options available in the Choose Task pane, you also can edit your site by dragging and dropping items within the site map on the left side of the FastSite window.

When you're ready to convert your files to Web pages (so that you can preview and then post them), click the Convert Files To Web Pages option on the Choose Task pane. You should also convert pages or sites that become out of date because they don't match their source files. FastSite uses a yellow circular icon to highlight files in the site map that need to be updated.

Previewing Web pages in FastSite

Always preview your Web pages before you post them to a Web server. Your pages must be converted to Web format before you can preview them. When you attempt to preview Web pages, FastSite gives you the option of converting them to Web format if you haven't already done so. To use FastSite to preview the pages in your Web site, follow these steps:

1. Select the site (or page) that you want to preview in the site map on the left side of the FastSite window.

2. Click the Preview Web Pages pane in the FastSite window. If you've already converted your files to Web format, you see the selected site (or page) on-screen. Skip to Step 4. Otherwise, if you see a message stating that the site preview is not available, click the Convert button and continue with Step 3.

3. In the Convert to Web Pages dialog box that appears, select the items that you want to preview and then click Convert. The Converting to Web Pages dialog box appears on-screen during the conversion process. (The conversion may take several minutes depending on your computer and the number of files that you are converting.)

4. In the site map on the left side of the FastSite window, click an item to display the corresponding Web page. You also can use the navigation keys at the top of your Web page to display other pages.

The following figure shows a preview of a Web page after it was converted from a 1-2-3 worksheet. If you want to preview your site in your default browser (rather than in FastSite's browser), click the Preview Web Pages In Browser link in the Choose Task pane.

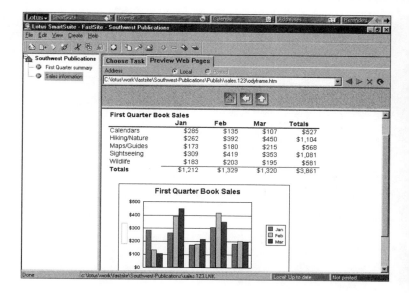

When you're ready to post your Web pages to a server, display the Choose Task pane in the FastSite window and click the Post Web Pages To A Server link. Follow the instructions in the Post to Server dialog box and click OK. If you need more information on this procedure, click the Help button in the dialog box or contact your network administrator or ISP.

Techie Talk

1-2-3: The spreadsheet application included with Lotus SmartSuite. 1-2-3 is covered in Part III of this book.

Action bar: A button bar in Approach that is located just below the SmartIcons. You can use action buttons to switch between different views, to create new records, and to find records.

Active cell: The current cell in 1-2-3, which displays the cell pointer. The contents of the active cell appear in the Contents box of the edit line.

Alignment: The horizontal or vertical positioning of data in a cell or document. You can change the alignment of data in all SmartSuite applications.

Approach: The database application included with Lotus SmartSuite. Refer to Part VI of this book for coverage on Approach.

Argument: An input (text, value, location, or condition) that you supply when entering a function or macro command.

Bubble help: Help information that appears in a bubble when you position the mouse pointer (and pause) over a SmartIcon or InfoBox tab.

Cell: The intersection of a row and a column in a 1-2-3 worksheet. You enter all 1-2-3 data in cells.

Cell comment: A note that you can attach to a cell in 1-2-3 to explain the contents of that cell.

Cell reference: Also called a *cell address*. Includes the sheet letter (optional), column letter, and row number of a 1-2-3 cell. For example, in the reference A:B12, A is the sheet letter, B is the column letter, and 12 is the row number.

Chart: A graphical representation of data in a SmartSuite application that can help you to identify trends and relationships in your data.

Clip art: Premade graphic objects that can be inserted in a SmartSuite document, most often in a Freelance Graphics presentation.

Clipboard: A temporary storage area that you can use to copy or cut data from one application and paste it into another application. The Clipboard is a Windows application and a feature of the operating system, and it can hold only one cut or copied object at a time.

Close button: The "X" icon that appears in the top-right corner of a window, dialog box, InfoBox, or application. Click the Close button to close the window, dialog box, InfoBox, or application.

Collection: A range of noncontiguous cells in 1-2-3. To select a collection, press Ctrl as you select multiple cells and/or ranges. Actions that you perform on a collection affect each cell in the collection.

Column: A vertical line of cells in 1-2-3, identified by a letter at the top of the column. Each worksheet includes 256 columns, lettered A to Z, AA to AZ, BA to BZ, and so on.

Contents box: In 1-2-3, displays the contents of the selected cell or the entry that you are typing or editing. The Contents box is the gray box located at the right end of the edit line.

Corex CardScan: A separate application, provided with SmartSuite Millennium Edition, that enables you to scan business cards into your address records in Organizer.

Database: A collection of information in Approach that is represented by fields and records of information.

Default: The standard settings that are normally used in an application. You can change many of the default settings used in SmartSuite applications.

Destination: An application or document that receives information from a source application or document. This term is typically used when you are cutting or copying data from one application (the *source*) and pasting it in another application (the *destination*).

Document: A Word Pro file that contains the text you type on-screen. Also used as a generic term to collectively refer to the files that you create in all SmartSuite applications (worksheets, presentations, and so on). Word Pro documents use the .LWP file extension.

EasyClip: A tool that lets you copy information from another program or location (such as an e-mail message) directly into Lotus Organizer.

Edit line: The row located just below the main menu in 1-2-3. The edit line includes the Selection indicator, Navigator, Function selector, Cancel and Confirm buttons, and the Contents box.

Expert (also called Ask the Expert): A new Help feature in 1-2-3 and Word Pro that enables you to type your own words to ask questions and find Help information on a particular feature or task.

FastSite: A new SmartSuite application that enables you to convert your existing SmartSuite documents to Web pages, preview the Web pages, and then post the pages to a Web server.

Field: The smallest unit of data in an Approach database, such as a Name, Address, or Zip code. Sometimes used to refer to a column in a 1-2-3 table.

Formatting: Enhancing the appearance of data in a document by changing fonts, number formats, alignment, colors, and other attributes (such as bold, italics, and underline).

Formula: A cell entry in 1-2-3 that performs calculations on numbers, text, or other formulas in a worksheet.

Freelance Graphics: The presentation graphics application included with Lotus SmartSuite. Refer to Part V of this book for more information on Freelance Graphics.

Function: A built-in formula in 1-2-3 that performs complex calculations for you automatically.

Function selector: Displays a drop-down list in 1-2-3, from which you can access a function that you want to insert in a cell.

Hyperlink: A cross-reference, or *link*, that lets you jump to a Web site, another file, or an object in the current document.

InfoBox: A special type of SmartSuite dialog box that provides a quick method of changing the properties of an object in the current file. The InfoBox remains on-screen as you make selections, enabling you to immediately see the effects of those changes in the document.

Insertion point: A blinking cursor that indicates where text will appear next when you type in a document.

Keyboard shortcuts: Also referred to as *shortcut keys,* these time-savers enable you to press a specified key combination to perform a task. For example, you can press Ctrl+S (hold down the Ctrl key and then press S) to save the current document.

Label: A text entry in 1-2-3, or text that explains parts of a chart. Also refers to text that is used to identify fields in the Design view of Approach.

Maximize/Restore button: The button that appears to the left of the Close button and enables you to maximize a window or application so that it fills the screen. Also used to restore a maximized window or application to its previous size (acts like a toggle).

Menu bar: The row of menu titles that appear directly below the title bar in all Windows applications. When you click a title in the menu bar, a full menu of choices appears.

Menu finder: A feature that shows you the equivalent menu commands in 1-2-3 and Word Pro to carry out tasks that you performed in another spreadsheet or word processor.

Minimize button: The button that appears to the left of the Maximize/Restore button. Click this button to store a window or application temporarily as a button at the bottom of the application's work area.

Named style: A collection of formatting attributes to which you assign a name. Named styles can be applied to a selection in a document.

Navigator: A button in the edit line of 1-2-3 that enables you to jump to and select a named range.

New Sheet button: The button located at the opposite end of the sheet tabs (on the right side of the screen) in 1-2-3. Used to insert a blank worksheet after the current sheet.

Number format: The formatting used to display numbers on-screen (with a percent sign, currency symbol, decimal places, and so on).

OLE: Stands for Object Linking and Embedding, a method used in Windows applications to share data among multiple applications.

Operators: Mathematical symbols that can be used in formulas, such as + (addition), - (subtraction), / (division), and * (multiplication).

Organizer: The personal information manager (PIM) application included with Lotus SmartSuite. Refer to Part VII of this book for coverage on Organizer.

Presentation: A collection of pages in a Freelance Graphics presentation that you save as a file. Freelance Graphics presentations use the .PRZ file extension.

Preview: A special on-screen view that lets you see how a document (or a portion of a document) will appear when printed.

Query: A method of displaying a subset of records in an Approach database based on criteria that you specify.

QuickDemos: Live demonstrations of actual tasks performed in a SmartSuite application. Search on QuickDemos in the Help system to access a list of QuickDemos that are available in that SmartSuite application.

Range: A contiguous, rectangular selection of cells in 1-2-3. To select a range, click a cell in one corner of the range and drag to the opposite corner. Actions that you perform on a range affect each cell in that range.

Range name: A name that you assign to a cell or range in 1-2-3. Range names can be used in place of cell references in commands, formulas, and functions.

Record: A complete set of related data in an Approach database, such as all the information for one employee in an employee database. Sometimes used to refer to a row in a 1-2-3 table.

Row: A horizontal line of cells in 1-2-3 that is identified by a number to the left of the row. Each worksheet includes 65,536 rows.

Save and Go: A feature that allows you to take your Freelance Graphics presentation on the road with you, even if the computer you will be using doesn't have Freelance Graphics loaded.

ScreenCam: A separate tool, included with SmartSuite, that enables you to capture "movies" of your computer screen. ScreenCam is useful for trainers.

Section tab: Folder-like tabs that you click to display a page of related information (such as the tabs that appear on the side of the Organizer notebook).

Selection: An item or area that is currently active in an application. Commands or tasks that you perform affect the current selection.

Selection indicator: Indicates the current cell address, selected range address, or selected range name in 1-2-3. The Selection indicator is the gray box located at the left end of the edit line.

Sheet scroll arrows: Arrow buttons in 1-2-3 that allow you to scroll the display of sheet tabs. These buttons, which appear to the right of the sheet tabs, are active only when some of the sheet tabs are not in view.

Sheet tab: A lettered tab that appears above the worksheet in a 1-2-3 workbook. A new workbook includes a single sheet tab, but you can add up to 255 more. Click a sheet tab to display that sheet. You can change the sheet tab letter to a descriptive name.

Shortcut menu: A context-sensitive menu that displays when you right-click in an application. The menu items change, depending on what you choose to right-click.

SmartCenter: The button bar that resides at the top of your screen to provide fast access to the SmartCenter applications, specific files, Internet sites, Help information, a calendar and address book, and more.

SmartFill: Automatically fills a 1-2-3 range, a Word Pro table or list, or a Freelance Graphics chart data sheet with a sequence of data, based on the data that you've already entered (such as numbers, dates, days of the week, and so on).

SmartIcons: Buttons that provide quick access to common commands and tasks in a SmartSuite application. The SmartIcons appear directly under the menu bar.

SmartLabels: Words (such as *Totals*) that 1-2-3 and Word Pro associate with certain formulas. SmartLabels enter formulas for you automatically in a 1-2-3 worksheet or Word Pro table.

SmartMasters: Preformatted custom templates provided in 1-2-3, Freelance Graphics, Approach, and Word Pro to give you a head start on creating a worksheet, presentation, database, or document.

Source: An application or document that sends information to a destination application or document. This term is typically used when you are cutting or copying data from one application (the *source*) and pasting it into another application (the *destination*).

Status bar: The bar at the bottom of the screen that includes buttons to provide quick access to formatting commands or other information relevant to the application.

Style Gallery: Style templates that you can use to quickly format tables in 1-2-3.

SuiteStart: A group of icons that enable you to start SmartSuite applications with a single click. These icons appear on the taskbar, at the opposite end from the Start button.

Title bar: The colored bar that appears at the top of an application, window, dialog box, or InfoBox. You can drag the title bar to move the object to another area of the screen (except when the window or application is maximized).

Toolbox: A group of icons in Freelance Graphics and Organizer that provide single-click access to common tools or tasks in that application.

Transitions: Visual effects that you apply to a Freelance Graphics presentation to make the presentation more interesting to the viewer.

URL: Stands for *Uniform Resource Locator,* another name for an Internet address.

Value: A numeric entry in 1-2-3 (including dates and times).

ViaVoice: A new application that allows speech recognition with Lotus Word Pro. You dictate into a microphone, and ViaVoice displays your speech in a document (without any typing).

Web page: A document that you use a Web browser to view. One or more Web pages can be called a *Web site.*

Web table: Data that you import from a Web page into a 1-2-3 table.

Word Pro: The word processing application included with Lotus SmartSuite. Part IV of this book covers Word Pro.

Workbook: A 1-2-3 file that can include up to 256 individual worksheets. Workbooks use the .123 file extension.

Worksheet: Also referred to as a *sheet.* A worksheet is the electronic spreadsheet, contained within a 1-2-3 workbook, in which you enter data. A new workbook includes only one worksheet, but you can add up to 255 more worksheets.

Zoom: Enlarges or reduces the on-screen display of a document. Zooming doesn't affect the appearance of printed documents.

Index

Symbols

* (asterisk) in 1-2-3 formulas, 60
*** (asterisks) in 1-2-3, 58, 72
@ sign preceding 1-2-3 functions, 61
@Function selector (1-2-3), 7,
   61–62, 191
^ (caret) in 1-2-3 formulas, 60
– (minus sign) in 1-2-3 formulas, 60
+ (plus sign) in 1-2-3 formulas, 60
/ (slash) in 1-2-3 formulas, 60

A

absolute references (1-2-3), 59
Action bar (Approach)
   on Approach screen, 11
   defined, 189
   Find Assistant button in, 143
   New Record button in, 141
active cell
   defined, 189
   on a 1-2-3 worksheet, 70
Actor Gallery, ViaVoice, 104
Add Clip Art Or Diagram to the
   Page dialog box (Freelance
   Graphics), 112
address, 1-2-3 cell, 59, 190
Address Preferences dialog box
   (Organizer), 153
address records in Organizer
   creating, 152–153
   editing, 154
   viewing, 153
Adobe Acrobat Reader 3.0, 21–22
Airline Guide, Official, 12
Alarm dialog box (Organizer), 151
alignment buttons (1-2-3), 40–41
Ami Pro users, help for, 26, 27
Anniversary section of Organizer, 148
apostrophes in 1-2-3, 59
application manuals, 21–22
appointments in Organizer
   editing, 150
   scheduling, 150–151
Approach
   Action bar, 11, 189
   creating new databases in, 132–137

defined, 10, 189
entering data in, 141–142
finding records in, 143–144
navigation SmartIcons, 142
new features in, 10
versus 1-2-3, 131
opening databases created in other
   applications from, 137
reports, 137–141
screen, 11
SmartMasters, 132, 135–137
sorting records in, 144–145
viewing options in, 132–133, 141
arguments in 1-2-3 functions, 61, 189
arranging windows in SmartSuite, 37
Ask the Expert (1-2-3, Word Pro)
   accessing and using, 22–23
   defined, 21, 191
asterisks in 1-2-3, 58, 60, 72
@AVG function (1-2-3), 63

B

background color for Word Pro text, 87
background color for worksheets,
   55–56
Backspace key (Word Pro), 82
birthdays in Organizer, entering, 148
blank databases (Approach), 133–135
boldface cells in 1-2-3, 56
boldface text in this book, 4
boldface text in Word Pro, 85
borders in 1-2-3, 55
borders in Word Pro, 85
Browse mode (Approach), 141
browsing Web with SmartCenter, 173
bubble help, 34, 189
bulleted lists (Word Pro), 78
business cards, scanning, 12, 190

C

Calendar Preferences dialog box
   (Organizer), 149
Calls section in Organizer, 154–155
CardScan, defined, 12, 190
caret symbol (1-2-3), 60
cascading windows, 37

(continued)

(continued)

views for, 126–129
as Web pages, 179–180
from Word Pro outlines, 168–169
preview, defined, 193
previewing
documents (Word Pro), 92–93
presentations (Freelance
Graphics), 122
reports (Approach), 140
Web pages in a browser, 179
Web pages in FastSite, 186–187
printing
documents (Word Pro), 93–94
envelopes (Word Pro), 94–95
Help topics, 23
labels (Word Pro), 95–96
Organizer data, 155–156
presentations (Freelance Graphics),
121–122
product updates, 22
reports (Approach), 140–141
worksheets (1-2-3), 68–70
proofing Word Pro documents, 96–98

Q

Query, defined, 193
QuickDemos
defined, 193
in Freelance Graphics, 26
in 1-2-3 and Word Pro, 25–26

R

range (1-2-3)
defined, 193
deleting contents from, 48–49
selecting, 70–71
sorting a range of data, 74
range name (1-2-3)
assigning, 66–67
defined, 193
Range Properties InfoBox (1-2-3)
Alignment tab, 40
Basics tab, 72–73
Color, Pattern and Line Style tab, 55, 56
Named Style tab, 58
Number Format tab, 58
Text Format tab, 57
record, defined, 193
records, Approach
deleting, 142
duplicating, 142
entering data for, 141–142
finding, 143–144

sorting, 144–145
Recycle Bin, Windows, 20
Redo feature (Word Pro), 36
reference, this book as a, 2
refreshing data in 1-2-3 Web table, 176
relative references (1-2-3), 59
removing hyperlinks, 173
removing SmartCenter from screen, 33
Report Assistant (Approach), 138–139
reports, Approach
creating, 137–140
previewing and printing, 140–141
resizing columns and rows (1-2-3), 72–73
resizing drawn objects (Freelance
Graphics), 114
restoring windows, 38
rotating data in a cell (1-2-3), 42
@ROUND function (1-2-3), 63
row (1-2-3), defined, 193
rows and columns in 1-2-3
deleting, 49
inserting new, 64
selecting, 71
sizing, 72–73
ruler in Word Pro, 101–102
Run Script dialog box, 168
running a screen show, 116–118

S

Save and Go (Freelance Graphics), 10, 123
Save As dialog box, 30
Save the Current File SmartIcon, 30
saving a file, 29–31
scanning business cards, 12, 190
scheduling appointments in
Organizer, 150–151
Scientific format (1-2-3), 72
screen show, running a, 116–118
ScreenCam
defined, 193
opening, 13
Section tab, defined, 193
selecting
cells in 1-2-3, 70–71
text in Word Pro, 98
worksheets in 1-2-3, 71–72
selection, defined, 193
Selection indicator (1-2-3), defined, 194
setting tabs in Word Pro, 101–102
sharing information
Clipboard for, 160
OLE for, 161–163
between 1-2-3 and Freelance
Graphics, 164–165
between 1-2-3 and Word Pro, 165–167

(continued)

Discover Dummies Online!

The Dummies Web Site is your fun and friendly online resource for the latest information about ...*For Dummies*® books and your favorite topics. The Web site is the place to communicate with us, exchange ideas with other ...*For Dummies* readers, chat with authors, and have fun!

Ten Fun and Useful Things You Can Do at www.dummies.com

1. Win free ...*For Dummies* books and more!
2. Register your book and be entered in a prize drawing.
3. Meet your favorite authors through the IDG Books Author Chat Series.
4. Exchange helpful information with other ...*For Dummies* readers.
5. Discover other great ...*For Dummies* books you must have!
6. Purchase Dummieswear™ exclusively from our Web site.
7. Buy ...*For Dummies* books online.
8. Talk to us. Make comments, ask questions, get answers!
9. Download free software.
10. Find additional useful resources from authors.

Link directly to these ten fun and useful things at **http://www.dummies.com/10useful**

For other technology titles from IDG Books Worldwide, go to
www.idgbooks.com

Not on the Web yet? It's easy to get started with *Dummies 101*®: *The Internet For Windows*® *95* or *The Internet For Dummies*®, 5th Edition, at local retailers everywhere.

Find other ...*For Dummies* books on these topics:

Business • Career • Databases • Food & Beverage • Games • Gardening • Graphics
Hardware • Health & Fitness • Internet and the World Wide Web • Networking • Office Suites
Operating Systems • Personal Finance • Pets • Programming • Recreation • Sports
Spreadsheets • Teacher Resources • Test Prep • Word Processing

The IDG Books Worldwide logo and Dummieswear are trademarks, and Dummies Man and ...For Dummies are registered trademarks
under exclusive license to IDG Books Worldwide, Inc., from International Data Group, Inc.

IDG BOOKS WORLDWIDE
BOOK REGISTRATION

Register
This Book
and Win!

We want to hear from you!

Visit **http://my2cents.dummies.com** to register this book and tell us how you liked it!

- ✔ Get entered in our monthly prize giveaway.
- ✔ Give us feedback about this book — tell us what you like best, what you like least, or maybe what you'd like to ask the author and us to change!
- ✔ Let us know any other ...*For Dummies*® topics that interest you.

Your feedback helps us determine what books to publish, tells us what coverage to add as we revise our books, and lets us know whether we're meeting your needs as a ...*For Dummies* reader. You're our most valuable resource, and what you have to say is important to us!

Not on the Web yet? It's easy to get started with *Dummies 101*®: *The Internet For Windows*® *95* or *The Internet For Dummies*, 5th Edition, at local retailers everywhere.

Or let us know what you think by sending us a letter at the following address:

...*For Dummies* Book Registration
Dummies Press
7260 Shadeland Station, Suite 100
Indianapolis, IN 46256-3945
Fax 317-596-5498

BUSINESS AND
GENERAL
REFERENCE
BOOK SERIES
FROM IDG

COMPUTER
BOOK SERIES
FROM IDG